BASEBALL AND NEW YORK: A POETIC WALK

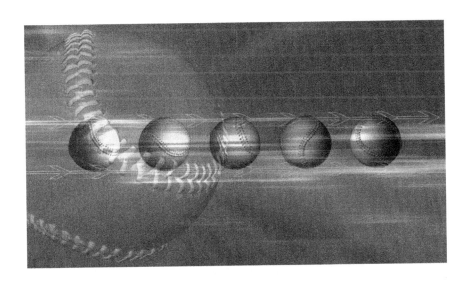

By
Randall Wayne McLean

For my wife, Linda, who has brought me more joy than all the ballgames ever played. Thank you for being the sweetest girl in the world and sharing your life with me. Without you, this book and my life are empty pages.

~

◆ FriesenPress

Suite 300 - 990 Fort St
Victoria, BC, Canada, V8V 3K2
www.friesenpress.com

Edited by Linda McLean
Front cover design by Randall and Linda McLean
Back cover design by Randall and Linda McLean
Back cover (About the Author) by Linda McLean
Additional photos from McLean family collection

ISBN
978-1-4602-7575-7 (Paperback)
978-1-4602-7576-4 (eBook)

1. Sports & Recreation, Baseball

Distributed to the trade by The Ingram Book Company

TABLE OF CONTENTS

POEMS

~

My life is like anyone else's. You're here, then you're gone.
I guess the only thing that separates me from many others
is baseball. You either get it or you don't. I get it! If you
don't, you should. It's what separates the men and women
from the boys and girls. I was one of the boys!

~ RWM

Baseball in Plumas, Manitoba in 1905. My Great
grandfather top row middle. Born 1875-1960.

~

INTRODUCTION

~

A few short years ago, in a rare moment of creativity, I found myself scribbling some thoughts down on paper. Until then, I had never reached a point in my mind where I even came close to entertaining thoughts of committing anything to print. The idea was precipitated more to galvanize a vault of personal memories best written out in longhand before they were forever forgotten. I've always had a special interest in the history of the world. Ancient Egypt, Greece, Rome, the Civil War, the World Wars, but baseball's rich history in particular has always fascinated me. The game of baseball not only gets my blood flowing but being an enthusiast, there was a natural progression for me to preserve any thoughts I might have on one of the rare topics I might, although remotely, know anything about. Not that I consider myself an authority, in fact, I'm far from it. Like many of us, I've read books by Tony LaRussa and George Will, books on Sandy Koufax and Ty Cobb to shortlist just a few. I came to realize a long time ago that there is so much more to learn. It is comforting to know that there will always be a fan base that will seek out the game's history with a passion that has helped to solidify baseball's foothold in our everyday lives. A baseball game is the only time in my life that I don't mind being wrong about what I think will happen or what I might predict will happen. If I could tell you what was going to happen, it wouldn't be much of a sport now would it? For me, the game of baseball is one of those rare topics where I don't feel out of my element should a discussion arise. I still have a long way to go to keep up with the hardcore fans, but I'm enjoying the ride. Getting there, after all, is half the fun.

At some point these mild ramblings began to take on a primitive form, and it was then that I decided that this could be my one and only chance to truly and at long last give something of myself back to the game that has treated me like royalty. It was of no consequence to me that the outside baseball world might, quite conceivably, never hear of me or from me. It would however, be of some small consolation to know that in my heart of hearts, my passion for the sport I love so much, would have once and for all been spelled out in ink, over perhaps, as I'm sure you will attest, for the love of our forests, far too many sheets of paper.

In a remote corner of my mind, behind a myriad of long forgotten cobwebs, there is a beacon of light that has been burning brighter with each written page. Deep down inside me there exists a faint hope or possibly a trace of wishful thinking that insists upon reaching out to you. With a humble whisper and perhaps a gentle inquiry, I ask you to read along with me. If one line of poetry or one forgotten memory stirs an emotion inside of you, even for one passing moment, then my ramblings have not been in vain. This was never, at any point, the ultimate goal for me as I fumbled with these musings. Nonetheless, I would be more than flattered if, but for one fleeting moment, you could sense in my words, a deep and profound love for the game of baseball. A treasure chest that has been thrown wide open, delivering upon me, a wealth of knowledge, smiles and memories. Securing a place in my heart for a game that will forever trickle through me. I am, perhaps one of the few, extremely fortunate individuals who was lucky enough to have found their calling. It would be a dream of mine to be of some small influence on anyone, who as of yet, hasn't been touched by the magic and wonders of the game of baseball. Along the way, my journey has taught me to embrace the game and in return, the game has embraced me. I am no doubt convinced that baseball will do the same for you!

~

THE WORLD IS WAITING

The words reside in my head somewhere,
Under dust, and scattered all over
Someday I'll make a clean sweep of it,
Play it out between hard covers.
The time has come to illuminate,
Let my light envelop the game
Baseball has always been there for me,
Now it's payback, without the pain.

I need to bleed out on paper,
Pure history in plain black and white
Legends arise amid colors and quotes,
From the left foul pole to the right.
Eight million stories that beg to be heard,
No excuse for slow off the mark
I'll pitch the tall tales of the underdog
And the heroes in every ballpark.

Baseball world, you've waited too long,
Immortality, it's me at last!
Its center stage, my number's been called
The spotlight, what more can I ask.
Memories unleashed, inspiration breaks free,
The new me demands a new order
Before you know it the side is retired,
Strike three, lights out, game over.

~ RWM

CHAPTER 1

~

BASEBALL RISING

The game of baseball has been an unwavering companion of mine for what is quickly becoming more years than I care to count. A loyal and close friend that has stood by me throughout my entire life. Through good times and bad. Recently I've had cause to ask myself an odd question. Is it possible that I've taken the game of baseball for granted all these years? Reaping the benefits without planting any future seeds? I considered the possibility, and realized I'd never actually thought about giving something of myself back to the sport that has meant so much to me. But realistically, what did I have to give? My love affair with the game had, for the most part, been a one-sided romance. All take with a minimal amount of give.

Looking back, I suppose I had been an ambassador for the game in my own quiet way. I'd always spread word of the game and its countless virtues to anyone who would listen. Anyone that knows me well knows the conversation begins and ends with baseball. I'm not as shallow as that sounds, but given the choice, baseball is what I prefer to talk about. Unfortunately, preference often takes a back seat for a sizeable portion of anyone's day as most of us already know. I do try to maintain the "baseball or nothing" stance day in and day out and what do you know? I am finally rewarded when October rolls around. The playoffs, where the postseason culminates with the pinnacle of all sports, the Fall Classic, the Holy Grail, the World Series! This event or at least the hype leading up to it, as any fan knows, is the ultimate in baseball feasting. A rare moment in time when all the tumblers of the universe fall into place. A window of opportunity thrown wide open to show the world what is possible. A sneak peek into what perfection in a sport truly looks like! A little over the top? Maybe, but please, just bear with me for a moment.

As with most sports, baseball regrettably has its fair share of detractors. I know, I know, it's hard to believe! It begins with those who insist on a theory wherein, saying you don't have the time to watch the game, amounts to an acceptable excuse. There are those who understandably admit to some confusion with the rules of the game. Perhaps for some, the season is too long; the athletes are overpaid, or the real shocker, the door closer, the conversation stopper, the naysayers who have the nerve to say the game is boring. Aaaghh!! Most sports mirror those very same characteristics on any given day so let's not get all excited and dog-pile on baseball. The magnificent Babe Ruth himself once said, "Baseball was, is, and always will be, to me, the best game in the world." The Babe, myself, and millions more like us worldwide share in this common belief.

This amazing fusion of sport, sportsmanship, athleticism, camaraderie, intellect and fan participation all thrown into the natural arena of the great outdoors is, in fact, almost impossible to overlook. Every household has its fair share of mirrors these days, so please, just take a quick look. Is the person looking back at you a future baseball fan? The person that has been standing out in the proverbial cold for far too long? Well, it's time to look ahead and do yourself this one eternal favor. Take the time, or better yet, make the time to investigate, because baseball as a spectator sport is one of the most relaxing games to wrap yourself around in this fine world of ours. The pleasures taken from the game don't always nor do they have to be exclusively based on the final score. Instead, immerse yourself within a family atmosphere. Treat your senses to the sights, sounds and smells of the ballpark. This will allow you to drop your worries at the gate and join the countless fans that turn out each day to reap the much-needed piece of mind acquired from spending the day with those you care most about.

For some, the game itself is secondary. More atmospheric conditions for bonding have yet to be discovered. A baseball game is the ideal setting for discovering the perfect mood. A generously offered gift which takes place in a thoughtfully sculpted park designed with only you in mind. Exquisitely manicured diamonds and emerald green fields wrapped up and played out for you under traditionally inspired azure blue skies. Just breathe it in! With a beer and hot dog in hand, peanuts or crackerjacks, you can take in a wealth of professional talent gathered from countries all around the world. Treat yourself to a game that has literally seen countries blossom around it. You will soon discover for yourself that the real game is not played on the field but is played out in each and every one of us.

Actor James Earl Jones' character, Thomas Mann, from the classic movie "A Field of Dreams," honored the game with this chant: "The one constant through all the years, Ray, has been baseball. Baseball has marked the time. This field, this game, is a part of our past Ray. It reminds us of all that once was good, and that could be again." I have watched it many times and his speech at that point in the movie has never failed to shake loose a few tears.

At first glance, the rules of the game appear to be plentiful but are basically easy enough for anyone to follow. As Willie Mays once said, "They throw the ball, I hit it, they hit the ball, I catch it." Perhaps that is oversimplifying the game a tad, but Willie's point is eloquently taken. As complex as the game can seem at the Major League level, its basic principles are easy enough to follow. Score more runs than the other team by the end of the game and you maintain bragging rights for at least one more day. These days, no matter the country or part of the world, countless throngs of youngsters are currently experiencing the game at every level. At the very least, they are staying out of trouble (at least until the game is over) and entertaining themselves with their own version of baseball.

Variations of the game are being played in the streets or fields of their respective homelands each and every day. Great Britain once laid claim to their own version of the sport in a popular old game they called Rounders. It was first referenced in 1744 in a book by John Newbery entitled, "A Pretty Little Pocket-Book", where it was called "base-ball". Who knew? Countries and continents worldwide are in the middle of a baseball renaissance. Central America as well as Venezuela for example, despite losing great numbers of their homegrown talent for much of the year to Major League Baseball, not only have players exploding on the professional scene, they are capably nurturing their own leagues.

Over the years, League expansion has never failed to open up avenues and opportunities and has enabled and encouraged the recruiting of new players and with it, new fans as well. Generating new revenue is always a plus and a necessity so it's quite conceivable that, as a result, the next new Major League franchise could realistically be awarded to a city in Mexico. This is more than a mere possibility as talks regarding such a move have apparently been discussed behind closed doors amongst baseball's many executives. Before the Montreal Expos folded their gloves and relocated to Washington D.C., the team made a closing statement for the future. They used a stadium in Puerto Rico as a home base for a portion of their games over the last two-year period of their existence. Indeed, the Major Leagues have already played pre-season games in front of wildly enthusiastic fans in standing room only stadiums across the ocean in Japan and south of the border in Mexico. Australia is next in line as the Arizona Diamondbacks and none other than the Los Angeles Dodgers agreed to open the 2014 Major League season in this remote but alluring continent. It's anybody's guess where the game will go from there.

Presently, there are Major League Baseball teams that employ players from far off countries such as Curacao, Aruba, Cuba, Italy and the Netherlands to name a few. The Dominican Republic and Puerto Rico have loaned out many of their immensely talented native sons which, in turn, has helped to promote and greatly improve the game in the U.S. as well as back home. The friendly neighbors to the North have successfully operated and nationally supported a team in Toronto since 1977. The only franchise at this writing, located outside of the United States. Montreal had its own franchise from 1969 through the 2004 season before relocating in Washington, D.C. Canada's immediate proximity to U.S. soil has had an influence on the game as well. Dozens of players have been drafted by Major League teams, with many more recently discovered prospects moving up through the ranks.

New arrivals on the baseball scene creating a stir and causing many scouts to stand up and take notice, are honing their skills in countries such as Russia and the aforementioned Italy. There are gloves, bats and balls quietly appearing in many other countries we will surely be hearing from very soon. The probability of these new players leaving their imprint on the game could be a few years down the road but the next shooting star from one of these emerging countries could be coming to a park near you in the very foreseeable future. Of course, anyone who follows the game at the Little League level is already aware of the electrifying presence of China, Chinese Taipei, South Korea, Taiwan, the Philippines and even Saudi Arabia as forces to be reckoned with. The United States has military bases situated throughout the world, and has for many years. That influence alone, could surely dictate the emergence of the next Joe DiMaggio, Roberto Clemente or Chan Ho Park from almost anywhere there are empty fields, baseball gloves and protective cups.

What can you say about the increasing interest of the game in Japan? The clubs in their professional leagues draw as well or even better than the greatest franchises Major League Baseball has to offer. The fans are knowledgeable, extremely passionate and literally ecstatic about their home teams and follow the players with a religious zeal. Their rosters are loaded with players that are quickly excelling at a level comparable to the high caliber of play now enjoyed by fans in North America. A point that is driven home with an exclamation mark as many of Japan's top stars are joining the growing legion of Korean players making their own mark on American soil.

The 2006 year heralded the beginning of a new era in international baseball with the World Baseball Classic boldly stepping up to the plate. The event is fully sanctioned by the professional leagues of all participating countries from around the world. Many Major League teams have expressed a concern regarding injuries or possible burnout for their own regular season but the tournament was held regardless in 2009 and once again in 2013. They contribute the best their nations have to offer in the true meaning of the term, "World Series." The success of this event has been clear and will continue to be regarded with hopeful eyes as the organizers wish this to be a recurring celebration for the month of March. Another fine example of the sport reaching out across oceans and borders to support and unify international baseball's community of players and fans alike.

One of the greatest men to ever grace our planet in recorded history, President Abraham Lincoln, had a baseball field constructed behind the White House. This was used almost exclusively for baseball games. Mr. Lincoln himself could often be seen playing baseball with kids on the front lawn of the presidential residence.

In the 1920s, former United States President Calvin Coolidge once boasted, "Baseball is our National game." While this may have been true at the time, it undoubtedly stands up under scrutiny today with many other countries now making the very same claim. President William Howard Taft also displayed a love for the game as seen in this quote taken from the Spalding Official Baseball Guide of 1911: "President Taft believes in baseball. He tells his friends that it is a past time worth every man's while and advises them to banish the blues by going to a ballgame and waking up with the enthusiasts of the bleachers who permit no man to be grouchy among them." Can't argue with the President!

It is of some significance that former President Andrew Johnson became the first U.S. leader to invite an entire baseball team to the White House, in that a somewhat modest fan such as myself, realizes, that I can't be far off the mark with my infatuations for the game. No less than recent President George W. Bush, became unashamedly giddy while anticipating a meeting with his modern day heroes. As a widely regarded baseball fan, President Bush once revealed, "One of the great things about living here (in the White House) is that you don't have to sign up for a baseball fantasy camp to meet your heroes. It turns out, they come here!"

As a matter of fact, since the early 1800s, the office of the U.S. Presidency has been overwhelmed by its own passion for America's game. Most schoolboys in the United States and many Canadians as well will no doubt recall a baseball poem entitled, "Casey at the Bat," by the late Ernest Lawrence Thayer. A classic in American literature, with the famous line sadly concluding, "...But there is no joy in Mudville—mighty Casey has struck out." In the early 1890s, a man named John Heydler, (who later became an umpire and president of the National League) made a comfortable living by reciting this historic poem on stage. He performed many public and private readings while traveling the countryside enjoying the benefits of a poem he hadn't written, but had memorized and repeated, literally thousands of times over the years. He received many personal invitations for his unforgettable recitations. Among them, none other than President Grover Cleveland. The President himself had summoned Heydler for one of his spirited renditions to take place in, where else but the Oval Office. Nice work if you can get it!

Since the early 1900s, many immigrant populations planting their roots in the USA found a way to initiate a path eventually leading them towards acceptance in not only baseball, but the country itself. The Italians, Poles, Irish and Latin Americans, to shortlist a few, broke ground with their dedication to the game and played with an unmatched enthusiasm which enhanced their overall play. The intense suffering that Jackie Robinson endured, paved the way for players of the immensely talented Negro Leagues to finally showcase their brilliance. He kicked the door down and left it wide open for future nations to charge through. They in turn, set the baseball world on fire while at the same time, taking a stand and representing themselves as deserving individuals as well. The possibilities are limitless as the baseball community continues to open its gates to countries reaching out to all four corners of the globe. So don't tell me the game is boring! Next to soccer, in popularity alone, acceptance of baseball is not only gaining momentum, it continues to boast a legion of fans in rapidly increasing numbers worldwide, with each passing year. As countless numbers have come to realize, the game eventually becomes a part of you. At this point, you have no choice but to relent, utterly helpless against its throes.

The time has finally come to give in if you haven't already. You would be wise to heed your senses and listen to a game that quietly yet insistently beckons you. You will not regret it!

Admittedly, a great number of the games' enthusiasts have preceded my modest participation. Of course I hold no patent on the game or the aura that surrounds it. Without being adamant or disrespectful, I have, in my own way, been endorsing the sport at almost every opportunity. To those who will listen and at times to those who pretend not to listen. Unfortunately, there are people with an "either you get it or you don't... and I don't," outlook. Simply put, the solution does not have to be so black and white. A number of people unaware of baseball's universal appeal refuse to venture out beyond their own backyards. And that's fine too. The game can be played there as well. Simply put, it's time to open up to baseball's infinite earthly qualities.

So before I belabor the point (is it too late?), I am asking those who haven't already, to open yourself up to a rare opportunity. Do not miss out on the infinite intrigue, the chess-like strategy that prevails with each inning. The serenity so easily absorbed and the pure bliss that will justify your time spent on this planet. If you miss out, it's your loss, and a big one at that! If there are lingering doubts or a big question mark, take a deep, deep breath and plunge headfirst regardless. If for no other reason, then do it for me. Come on! Where's the trust? Tell yourself, "this is the day I finally open up to the many life-altering possibilities that await me in the profoundly, beguiling game being played on diamonds worldwide." You might want to tone that down a bit, but hopefully my sincerity speaks for itself.

Discover a lifelong reward, on the cutting edge of personal gain, which will continually refresh your inner being. Listen to those who have inherited the proven benefits of relaxation at a very high standard. Strive to achieve peace of mind and at the same time, dive in and educate yourself in the game's rich past. An enchanting history that patiently awaits your arrival. Accessible on demand to one and all. A history currently and eternally establishing itself as we speak. It unfolds each and every day, so on *this* day, clear your slate and check your local listings for a game nearest you! You won't regret it!

~

CHAPTER 2

~

WHAT'S THE CATCH

"There's a long drive way back in center field...way back, back! It is...oh, what a catch by Mays! The runner on second (Larry Doby), is able to go to third. Willie Mays... just brought this crowd to its feet...with a catch...which must have been an optical illusion to a lot of people. Boy!"

Jack Brickhouse of NBC-TV

Willie Howard Mays, Jr. was born in Westfield, Alabama, a small steel-mill town on the outskirts of Birmingham, on May 6, 1931. Raised by a mother who excelled in local track and field events, and a father who played outfield for the Birmingham Black Barons of the Negro National Leagues, Willie was the first of twelve children. He was to star himself for those same Black Barons in 1947, the first professional team on which he played. It was while playing for the Barons that Willie's talent rose to the top. He excelled in every facet of the game, and would continue to do so throughout what was to be an exceptional and in many ways, unprecedented Hall of Fame career.

Willie Mays, Sr., perhaps saw this passion for the game emerge in his son some years earlier. Before young Willie could even walk, his father would roll a baseball back and forth to him. When dad stopped – Willie cried.

His father once commented, "I never saw a boy who loved baseball the way Willie always did."

Willie Mays' talents did not go unnoticed. When Jackie Robinson was called upon to play for the Brooklyn Dodgers in 1947, he became the first black player in Major League baseball. This opened the door for a multitude of the multi-talented Negro League players to finally play professional baseball and show off their skills. Four years later, in 1951, Mays was summoned to the New York Giants from Minnesota, while playing for his Minor League team at the time, the Minneapolis Millers. Robinson broke down the barrier and as a result received untold abuses from fans and players alike. He paved the way for many young players from the Negro Leagues, and Willie Mays never forgot it. *"Everytime I look at my pocketbook I see Jackie Robinson."* A simple statement that spoke volumes for the gratitude Willie felt. He still endured many of the same abuses suffered by Jackie, but like Robinson, he kept his emotions well hidden. Except on the ballfield! He acquired the nickname the "Say Hey Kid" from the enthusiastic way he greeted all his teammates.

However, the confidence he played with in the Minor Leagues had subsided somewhat once he was called up. He expressed his apprehensions about the ability to hit Major League pitching to then Giant's manager Leo Durocher. Durocher inquired as to what his batting average was for his Minor League team, and Mays replied .477. "Do you think you can hit two-fucking-fifty for me?" With that, Mays was headed for the East Coast.

Durocher had many rough edges and rubbed a lot of the people the wrong way, but Willie and Leo respected each other and were always compatible. Willie always addressed him as "Mr. Leo." After going hitless in his first twelve at bats, it was no secret that Willie was having a tough time at the plate. Again, he approached Durocher with doubts about his ability to hit the elite pitching in the Majors, but the manager told him he was his center fielder no matter what he hit. Mays had one hit in his first 26 at bats, but exploded with the coach's new found confidence in him.

Willie always had a flair for the dramatic and that first hit was no exception. In his thirteenth at bat, on May 28, 1951, he hit a towering home run off of future Hall of Famer Warren Spahn that cleared the left field roof of the Polo Grounds in New York. When the home run was brought up after the game, the reporters asked Spahn what had happened. "Gentleman," he said, "for the first 60 feet that was a hell of a pitch". Willie would go on to hit 17 of his 660 home runs off of Spahn. The most he hit off of any pitcher. Later Spahn remarked, "He was something like zero for twenty-one the first time I saw him. His first Major League hit was a home run off me and I'll never forgive myself. We might have gotten rid of Willie forever if I'd only struck him out." Mays went on to win Rookie of the Year in 1951 with 20 home runs, 68 RBI and a .271 batting average in 121 games, and never looked back.

Known around the League as much for his defense as well as his bat, Willie made some remarkable catches in center field over the years. Durocher had always maintained that a player had to have the five main tools at the ready to be considered one of the best. Willie was the best he had ever seen. He could run, throw, field, hit and hit for power. Very few players in the history of the game had it all, but Willie Mays most definitely did! As Durocher once proclaimed, "If he could cook, I'd marry him."

The Korean War had started in 1950 and once again, Americans were called upon to fight for their country. Willie played only 34 games for the Giants in 1952 and missed all of the 1953 season due to military service. Mays returned in 1954 with a vengeance. He won the MVP award that year and returned to play in what was to be a memorable World Series in more ways than one. His statistics that year more than solidified him as one of the game's finest. Along with a .345 average, he hit 41 home runs, drove in 110, and finished first in the League with 119 runs scored. It was to be the first of twelve straight years in which he would score over 100 runs.

Mays and his New York Giants lost the World Series to the Yankees in 1951 but returned to the Fall Classic in 1954 to face the Cleveland Indians. Cleveland was coming off a year in which they had set a mark for most wins by an American League team with 111, against 43 losses, for a .721 winning percentage. The Indians boasted a pitching staff that included the extraordinary Bob Feller, Mike Garcia, Bob Lemon, Hal Newhouser and Early Wynn. They seemed unbeatable.

During the first game in New York, Mays was to make what historians now simply refer to as "The Catch." Perhaps the greatest catch in World Series history, but for Willie, just one in a string of many. As Mays himself would say, "When they throw the ball, I hit it. When they hit the ball, I catch it." A unique way of simplifying the game! Infielder Vic Wertz had given the Indians a 2-0 lead in the first inning with a two-run triple off the right field wall, against Giants' pitcher Sal Maglie. When Wertz came to bat in the top of the eighth inning with men on first and second, and nobody out, the game was tied 2-2. Durocher took Maglie out of the game and put a small left-hander, by the name of Don Liddle in to replace him. On the very first pitch from Liddle, Wertz connected. It must have felt good! He drove the ball soaring into the deepest part of the cavernous Polo Grounds, which at that time, measured in excess of 460 feet. Because of the sheer depth of the wall and the electrifying quickness of Mays, it always seemed that he was playing a shallow centerfield. Willie was well aware of his own speed, and although Wertz's hit appeared to be a sure home run, instinct took over and he turned and ran. Rumor had it that Mays liked to wear his hat one size too small, making for a more dramatic looking catch when it flew off his head while on the run. No theatrics were needed for this grab. With his back completely turned away from home plate, two hands rose up to make the most incredibly amazing catch. The 52,751 fans watched in disbelief, not quite comprehending what they had just witnessed. To complete the play, and knowing exactly where he was, Willie stopped, planted, and threw a bullet back to the infield, twisting and falling to the dirt in the process. Not quite believing themselves what had just happened, the runner on second, outfielder Larry Doby could only retrace his steps, tag up and go to third. The runner on first quickly sprinted back to his bag and could only watch as the ball rocketed back into the infield. One out!

As Don Liddle had only been in the game to pitch to this one batter, Durocher made his way out to the mound pulling him for the next reliever Marv Grissom. As history and rumor would have it, Liddle walked off the field, tossed the ball to Grissom and quipped, "Well, I got my man." There are baseball historians who maintain the line was delivered in the locker room as Mays, Durocher and Liddle continued their discussion of the game afterwards. Durocher spread the word of the remark, but regardless of where it was delivered, Liddle's sense of humor was timely. Grissom got the remaining two outs of the inning and the Giants went on to win the first game of the Series on Dusty Rhodes' game winning, three-run home run off of Bob Lemon in the bottom of the tenth inning. Monty Irvin had played left field beside Willie Mays for the Giants that day and got an up-close look at his historic catch. He had this to say: "Now on the way in after we got the third out, I ran in with him, you know, so I said to him, 'I didn't think you were gonna get to that one'. He said, 'You kiddin'? I had it all the way!'"

Mays didn't seem to know what all the fuss was about. He had made great plays before, and he would no doubt make them again. Before Rhodes' homer had finally won the game, Wertz had once again come to the plate with the game still tied 2-2. He drove another shot to left center off Grissom that looked like a possible inside-the-park home run. Mays speared the ball on one bounce and threw a dart back to the infield, holding Wertz to a double. Willie confided that he considered that play much more difficult than "The Catch". But as he once said about his own defensive abilities, "I don't compare 'em, I just catch 'em!" Sounds very humble for a man that once boasted, "I think I was the best baseball player I ever saw!"

It didn't seem fair to the other ballplayers for a man to have that much talent. The first game of the 1954 World Series produced a defensive gem that will forever live in infamy. But the catch itself was apparently not Willie's best as he himself states, "The catch off Bobby Morgan in Brooklyn was the best catch I ever made." It was a diving backhand of a line drive in September, 1951. After making that catch, Mays landed on his chest and knocked himself out as he bounced into the concrete wall in Ebbets Field. The left fielder, Henry Thompson, ran over and held up Willie's glove hand with the ball in it, and only then, did the umpire signal Morgan out! Another favorite of Willie's was his catch off the bat of Ted Williams in the 1955 All-Star game. Over the years, the list continued to go on and on. As one sportswriter said, "He should play in handcuffs to even things up!"

Willie is now considered "the greatest living ballplayer" as of this writing. Many wonder what took so long. When baseball's elite were polled after Joe DiMaggio's death, to see who would now hold the title, Hall of Fame pitcher Bob Gibson remarked, "You're assuming DiMaggio *was* the greatest living ballplayer!" A sentiment apparently Gibson didn't share. Whenever the topic arises, one thing is for sure. Willie's name is there among the top three: Mays, Mantle and DiMaggio. The debate continues.

To support the Mays contention, his statistics certainly back up "the greatest living ballplayer" status. He retired after the 1973 season with 660 home runs which, at the time, was third on the all-time list behind Babe Ruth, with 714, and Hank Aaron, who had just passed Willie in 1972, with a still running total. In a 22-year career, Mays accumulated 1,902 RBI and scored 2,062 runs, while finishing with a .302 batting average. Mays was a twelve-time Gold Glove winner, and played in an astonishing 24 All-Star games. An odd statistic considering he only played 22 years and wasn't selected in his first two. In clarification, for four straight years, starting in 1959, Major League baseball played All-Star games in two different cities, in an attempt to help establish funds for the newly-formed players' pension plan. This enabled Willie to perform in an incredible 24 All-Star games. In addition to his 1954 MVP, he collected one more Most Valuable Player award, that coming in 1965, while playing in California.

Following the 1957 season the New York Giants became the San Francisco Giants, moving to the West Coast for the 1958 season, the same year the Brooklyn Dodgers became the Los Angeles Dodgers. Although neither of the franchises could ignore the added revenue from relocation, or the star power of the "Say Hey Kid," fans in San Francisco never took to Willie the way the fans in the Polo Grounds did. It would not be stretching the truth to say Mays would have preferred to stay in New York, but you'd never know from the statistics he accumulated in his new home ballpark. One of the amazing records Willie Mays owns still stands today. He is the only outfielder to have over 7,000 put-outs, finishing with 7,095, in a career that ended up back in where else, but New York. He was traded back to the Big Apple and the New York Mets part way through the 1972 season, and finally retired after losing in the 1973 World Series in seven games to Charlie Finley's Oakland Athletics.

Willie Mays currently has a lifetime appointment as special assistant to the president of the San Francisco Giants. Mays is the godfather of former superstar Barry Bonds, whose father was a longtime teammate of his while playing for the San Francisco Giants. Willie Mays' talent and enthusiasm for the game can best be summed up in his own words:

> *"I can never understand how some players are always talking about baseball being hard work. To me, it's always been a pleasure, even when I felt sort of draggy after a double header."*

In the words of Sports Illustrated columnist Roy Blount, Jr.:

"When Mays is poised in the outfield or at bat, he seems more eager or anxious than anybody else. He has the air of that kid in a pickup game who has more ability and fire than the others, and wishes intensely that they would come on and play right and raise the whole game to a level commensurate with his own gifts and appetites."

Willie Mays was inducted into the Hall of Fame in 1979, his first year of eligibility. Mays will always be recognized and remembered for the gifts he displayed on the field and at the plate, but when most of us hear the name Willie Mays, we will always remember "The Catch." Perhaps the words of the man who hit the ball, Vic Wertz, captured the sentiments most of us feel when we are reminded of this amazing feat:

"I don't think I ever hit a ball better or harder than that one. Yes, I know I've put balls on the roof at Briggs Stadium at Detroit, and hit some other real smashes, but this drive, which just ended as a big out, was tagged as well or better than any of them. I never thought Mays had a chance to get the ball, but he did!"

~

THE CATCH

The first page was turned at the Polo Grounds
History will remember "Say Hey"
With the crack of the bat, he inhaled the sound
And triggered his long resume.

A shot hit by Wertz, a man in his prime
Two hands rose up through the haze
Chased down and caught in the webbing of time
And a glove inscribed, "Willie Mays."

With ease, he teased, a cinch all along
In hindsight, I guess we all knew
The catch alone, like the perfect song
But still, Willie turned and threw.

Cleveland stood pale, visibly amazed
For surely they'd won the ballgame
Until "24" took flight that day
And immortalized his name.

Irvin, in left, had now seen it all
"The best ever", had run the ball down
You can run all the way, as Monte recalled
To a place we call Cooperstown.

Baseball to many was merely a word
Until that September day
The catch lived on but rumors were heard
The Giants would have a short stay.

The team moved west, confirming all fears
New Yorkers still aren't done cryin'.
But Willie would have you shed not a tear
For he will forever remain a Giant!!

~ RWM

CHAPTER 3

~

A LETHAL DOSE

The Waner brothers were born in the small farming community of Harrah, Oklahoma. Paul Glee Waner came into this world on April 16, 1903, and younger brother Lloyd James Waner followed on March 16, 1906. The brothers went on to play twenty and eighteen years, respectively, of professional baseball and became the only two brothers voted into the Baseball Hall of Fame.

The boys' unique nicknames were more than justified and stuck with them throughout their long and prosperous careers. Paul acquired the name "Big Poison" for his game-breaking ability to hit doubles and triples into the gap. Lloyd, a fine ballplayer himself, was destined to become "Little Poison" if, for no other reason, than being Paul's younger brother. By the end of their storied careers, they had combined hits totaling 5,611, a record that still stands to this day. A record that might never be broken. The Waner brothers had more hits than Vince, Dom, and Joe DiMaggio, and 500 more than their nearest competitors, the Alou brothers, Felipe, Matty and Jesus. They played on many great Pirate teams, but managed only one World Series appearance in 1927, where they lost in four straight games to Babe Ruth and the New York Yankees. Lloyd hit for a .400 average in that Series and Paul followed at .333. They had many great teammates in

Pittsburgh over the years with names that included future Hall of Famers, Arky Vaughan, Pie Traynor (apparently so named for his affinity for pastries), and Waite Hoyt.

Lloyd played a stellar center field and possessed exceptional speed. Like Fred Lynn, who debuted for the Boston Red Sox in 1975, his rookie year was perhaps his best. That year was 1927 when he batted .354, while pounding out 223 hits and was second in the League with 133 runs scored. Older brother Paul set a fine example that same year as he batted .380 with 237 hits and 131 RBI. Totals which were to garner Paul his one and only MVP award. Lloyd went on to play eighteen years in the Major Leagues, collecting 2,459 hits in 1,993 games. He had only one All-Star selection but somehow only struck out an incredibly miniscule 173 times in his career. During a ten-year period from 1936 to 1945, he was to strike out only 55 times. To put those numbers in perspective, that is approximately one strike out per month. He must have had an incredible eye for the ball. It was his quickness in the outfield and on the bases, which caught the attention of many a manager. One of his many tools which were used to help change the face of the game at that time. Teams began searching for speed, as well as a good glove and bat. Skilled defensive play would become a new weapon and a welcome addition to offensive production for winning ballgames. Though the Waners were slightly built, both brothers achieved unequalled success on the diamond. In 1927 alone, they accumulated a staggering 460 hits between them. A manager's dream!

Although there seems to be more recorded information available for Paul, perhaps for his exploits off the field, the stories never came close to overshadowing his accomplishments on the field. Paul loved to have a drink, and never downplayed the fact. According to Lloyd, Paul believed he was a better ballplayer if he was relaxed. There was no better way to relax than having a few drinks, seemed to be Paul's way of thinking. Casey Stengel once said of him, "He had to be a graceful player, because he could slide without breaking the bottle on his hip." You can't argue with big brother's success.

In twenty years on the ball field, he was to amass 3,152 hits in 2,549 games, had a lifetime batting average of .333, four All-Star selections, three batting titles, 1927 (.380), 1934 (.362), and 1936 (.373), and as earlier mentioned, won the MVP in 1927. In 1942, he became just the sixth player to collect 3,000 hits. He was probably the only player, according to legend, to turn down an official base hit. This particular game came against Cincinnati at a time when he was stuck at 2,999 hits. While trying to cover second base on a hit and run, Cincy shortstop Eddie Joost was caught going the wrong way on a grounder hit by Paul. Joost tried to stretch back for the ball, got a glove on it, but couldn't make the play. The official scorer raised a finger indicating a hit, which was met by a strong protest from none other than the hitter himself. He waved his arms furiously and yelled "No, no, no" at the press box as the umpire retrieved the ball, thinking it a keepsake. Shortly after, he got his wish as the scorer reversed his decision and Paul got his 3,000th hit two days later. This time it was a clean single.

In 1938, thinking the Pirates had a clear shot at the World Series title, the team apparently asked Paul to quit drinking which had become quite a well-known habit. Paul reluctantly agreed, but when his average dipped to .241, manager Pie Traynor began to buy him drinks! He finished the year at a paltry.280, which would turn out to be his only season as a Pirate in which he batted under .300. Is there a valuable lesson in there for all of us? Maybe just Paul! For his career, he batted over .300, fourteen times, including twelve consecutively.

Paul and Lloyd wreaked much havoc upon opposing pitchers, so the "Poison" monikers were a suitable choice. Taking the accent into account, it was once stated that the word "poison" was Brooklynese for "person." As one fan in Ebbets Field once complained, "Every time you look up those Waner boys are on base. It's always the Little Poison on thoid and the Big Poison on foist."

The boys from Oklahoma enjoyed incredible careers. The fact that two brothers could play on the same team and carry such talent was as much of a thrill for them as it was for Major League Baseball. We might not see the likes of it again. Paul Waner was inducted into the Baseball Hall of Fame in 1952. He died in Sarasota, Florida, on August 29, 1965. Lloyd Waner was voted into the Baseball Hall of Fame by the Veteran's Committee in 1967. He died in Oklahoma City, Oklahoma, July 22, 1982.

~

THE POISON BROTHERS

Any mother would love them both
No matter the career they'd chosen
But how was Mrs. Waner to know
They'd be famous in measures of poison.

Two kids from South Oklahoma
In baseball they'd shared an endeavor
Pittsburgh was home for sixteen years
But they'll share the same outfield forever.

Paul earned his title Big Poison
He played it for all it was worth
Lloyd was so-named for one reason
You'd think they'd been chosen at birth.

The boys were good, but Paul was bad
Saw the world through bloodshot eyes.
He loved the game, and gave it all he had
Lloyd starred under clear blue skies.

Forbes had the brick and the ivy
With poison between the lines
Paul was the mark of consistency
Batting three hundred, fourteen times.

As brothers, their record stands fast
A moment in time for the Waners
Each game was played like their last
In a lineup shared with Pie Traynor.

Many great men have played the game,
Very few, are Hall of Famers.
Ladies and gentlemen, your attention please
I present Paul and Lloyd, The Waners!

~ RWM

CHAPTER 4

~

BAKER BOWL

"Several rules of stadium building should be carved on every owner's forehead. Old, if properly refurbished, is always better than new. Smaller is better than bigger. Open is better than closed. Near beats far. Silent visual effects are better than loud ones. Eye pollution hurts attendance. Inside should look as good as outside. Domed stadiums are criminal."

- How Life Imitates the World Series

In the early days of ballpark construction, the contours of the home field were often dictated by the urban sprawl surrounding it. Many of the old ballparks that have survived today are witness to this fact. Boston's Fenway Park had a 37-foot wall with a 23-foot high screen built because of its close proximity to Lansdowne Street. The wall was to even things out for batters hitting to a short left field, the screen was to protect windows in the buildings across from the outer wall. Most ballparks were especially unique as the builders found themselves having to shoehorn the fields in to the dimensions given them. This accounted for the short right field fence in Brooklyn's Ebbets Field, and the odd-shaped Griffith Stadium in Washington. Local landowners in the nation's capital refused to sell their property around the newly-built Griffith, thus making it 407 feet to left field, 421 to center and a mere 320 down the right field line. A 30-foot high concrete wall stood out to all who attended the games, but still found itself five feet closer and seven feet shorter than Fenway's Green Monster.

Baker Bowl was no different in its abnormalities. Officially named National League Park in its inception, it was often called Huntingdon Street Grounds for the street which it bordered upon. The park, built at a cost of $101,000, opened on April 30, 1887, to much revelry before catching fire and burning to the ground in 1894. The new rebuilt version was made almost entirely of steel, brick, and concrete to guard against future fires. It was, at the time, the first park in the U.S. to use the cantilever design, which, for the most part, gave fans an unobstructed view of the game. In 1913, the field became known as Baker Bowl, named after former New York Police Commissioner, William F. Baker who had purchased the club which he owned until his death in 1930.

Despite some small changes in the early years, the outfield distances stabilized in the 1920s, making it 341 feet down the left field line, a healthy 408 feet to center, but only a paltry 280 down the right field line, stopping just short of Broad Street. Something had to be done to compensate for the short porch in right, so during its formative years, a 40-foot high wooden fence was erected (raised to 60 feet in 1929) and ran from the clubhouse in center-field to the right field foul line. Because of the wall's enticement for the hitters playing in Philadelphia's ballpark, Baker Bowl was the butt of many jibes. It was often called "tiny" and labeled a "cigar box" or "band box." The first game ever played here served testament to the constant ribbing it received. Although the Phillies prevailed, the score was a laughable 19-10 over the New York Giants. Fifty-one years later, those same Giants would avenge this loss beating the home team Phils 14-1 in the last game played at the grossly outdated Baker Bowl. The uncommon dimensions obviously didn't escape the attention of the sportswriters of that day. Predictably, right field took the brunt of it. Local scribe Red Smith would later write, "It might be exaggerating to say the outfield wall cast a shadow across the infield, but if the right fielder had eaten onions at lunch, the second baseman knew it."

Because of the ridicule the park received, many of the home team Phillies' accomplishments were received with raised brows. Unfortunately,

Chuck Klein was foremost among them. Klein toiled for the Phils for most of his eighteen plus years in the Major Leagues, starring as a rookie in 1928. During his six prime years with Philadelphia, from 1928 to 1933, he led the League in hits and doubles twice and home runs four times. Although many alluded to the small confines at Baker Bowl for Klein's successes, he reached a goal few Major Leaguers have ever achieved. He collected four home runs in one game, performing this rare feat at spacious Forbes Field in Pittsburgh, not the "cigar box" as many believed Baker to be. Klein finished his illustrious career with a .320 average and exactly 300 homers. In 1930, his most productive season, he hit .386 with 40 home runs and 170 RBI, yet failed to lead the League in any one of those categories. He was the National League MVP in 1932 and won the Triple Crown the following year. Klein still holds the modern-day record for most assists by a National League outfielder with 44 in 1930. Skeptics overlooked Chuck Klein's accomplishments because he played on a field which, to many, housed a ballplayer perceived to be less than worthy of a baseball legend. He was passed over for entry into the Hall of Fame for many years until the Veterans Committee, at long last, recognized his achievements and finally voted him into the Hall in 1980.

Grover Cleveland ("Old Pete") Alexander had no such difficulties in his quest for immortality. Although playing in a park which favored left-handed batters, the right-handed pitcher won thirty-one games in 1915, thirty-three in 1916 and thirty more games in 1917. He didn't exactly take the year off in 1914, winning twenty-seven games for these same Phils, which to some extent paled in comparison to the following three seasons. His sixteen shutouts in 1916 and four one-hitters in 1915 are still Major League highs. The prowess he exhibited on the mound in the early years of Baker Bowl sent the Phillies to the World Series in 1915 and helped the city gain prominence in the eyes of the baseball world. The strange yet colorful owner, Bill Veeck once said of Alexander, "Deplore it if you will, but Grover Cleveland Alexander drunk was a better pitcher than Grover Cleveland Alexander sober." Despite bouts of alcoholism and the burden of carrying with him the horrors of combat in WWI, he won an incredible 373 games spanning a brilliant twenty-year career. These statistics so impressed the voters, that Grover Cleveland Alexander was ushered into the Hall of Fame in 1938, making him one of the first twelve players chosen to reach this elite status.

Legendary sportswriter Grantland Rice summed up Alexander's career this way: "He could pitch into a tin can. His control was always remarkable—the finest I have ever seen." Keeping on this historical note, baseball enthusiasts will be interested to learn that Babe Ruth, as a member of the Boston Braves, played his last game at Baker Bowl in 1935. After a first inning groundout to the infield, the Babe took himself out of the first game of a doubleheader and never played professional baseball again.

Speaking of the Babe, baseball fans have always been enamored with the home run ball, but few will ever undermine the importance of pitching. In 1930, Baker Bowl carried with it some strange occurrences. Philadelphia had an astounding team batting average of .315, but ultimately finished forty full games out of first place, obviously a last place finish. They scored an amazing 543 runs in 77 home games that year, but relinquished a staggering 644 runs to the opposition, an average of 15 runs per game by both teams. Neither the 1927 nor the 1961 Yankee teams scored with such abandon as the 543 runs tallied by the Phils that year. The park was not without its quirks, but the fans nonetheless received entertainment by the bucketful.

Did I mention quirks? Oddly enough, the blueprints for the field put the clubhouse in center field, which rose some 35 feet from ground level and boasted a dozen sizeable arched windows. Cosmetically, it was a nice touch had it not been for the left field bleachers, which didn't exactly run flush with the clubhouse. Instead, it extended a number of feet in front of it, creating an odd slant and an extended alleyway through to the distant center field wall. With the 40-foot wooden wall in right connecting to the eventual concrete clubhouse, any balls hit hard enough to this abstract outfield would have resembled more a pinball machine than a natural carom. If that wasn't enough, for many years, an inclined warning track bordering the field made the last few feet for an outfielder chasing an errant ball a slight uphill climb. To make matters even worse, the Philadelphia and Reading Railroad ran through a tunnel underneath the deepest part of the park crating a very noticeable hump in center field. It is not known whether management attempted to acquire mountain goats to navigate the rise, but the stadium groundskeepers did in fact house three sheep in living quarters beneath the bleachers. The grounds crew only had to bring the sheep out after and between games to keep the infield and the outfield grass trimmed. A novel approach, but in its day, seemed appropriate.

Thankfully, the park was not without partial glories. As earlier mentioned, Baker Bowl was home to the 1915 World Series, which was then a five-game affair. The Phillies took the Series to the limit before losing the deciding game to the Boston Red Sox. In an effort to gain additional revenue from the playoffs, owner Bill Baker installed extra bleachers in front of the right field wall. An odd decision for a wall that was only 280 feet to begin with. As Baker Bowl's fate would have it, the ground rules that covered these extra seats, backfired for the home team. Boston's Harry Hooper bounced two long fly balls into the newly constructed stands that were eventually ruled home runs in a 5-4 win over the puzzled Phillies. Let's hope the monetary gains were worth it, as the Phillies and their fans in this particular park, never again witnessed World Series action. Many historians and students of the game will no doubt remember the Hilldale Daisies of Darby, PA, and the many Negro League ballgames played at Baker Bowl in the 1920s and 1930s. In fact, Negro League World Series games were played there in 1924 to 1926. With great fan support.

On a tragic note, in 1903, only eight short years after the park had been rebuilt in 1895, and after a fire the year before, the bleachers on the third base side collapsed. As a game was in progress at that time, the stands were unfortunately filled and eleven baseball fans were killed in the fall, with another 200 receiving injuries. To compound Baker's troubled history, almost 24 years later on May 14, 1927, a portion of the right field stands gave out as well, causing numerous serious injuries. Fortunately, the 1927 tragedy resulted in no loss of life.

In an era when many of the new ballparks being built housed upwards of 40,000 to 50,000 fans, Baker Bowl never held more than 20,000. The lack of revenue over the years created rundown conditions in the maintenance department, and as a result, attendance in the 1930s dwindled to an average of a mere 2,500 fans. Upgrades in the interior of the park suffered as well. A Philadelphia sportswriter once wrote, "National League players will be pleased to learn that the visiting dressing room at Baker Bowl is being completely refurbished for next season—brand new nails are being installed on which to hang their clothes." The humor was well noted, but for the unfortunate professional ballplayers on the Philadelphia Phillies, the shots ricocheted from the newspapers to their wounded pride. It had to be excruciating for the home team, to play their hearts out and have not only their home confines ridiculed, but the honest efforts they displayed on the field as well. In those same 1930s, an advertisement splashed across the 40-foot wall in bold letters, boasted gleefully, "The Phillies Use Lifebuoy." The fans recited these same words but were quick to add, "but they still stink."

This was literally the writing on the wall. A few blocks away, Connie Mack's Philadelphia A's were playing fine baseball in Shibe Park. This was the first stadium ever constructed exclusively of concrete and steel. Named after owner Ben Shibe, the park was built in 1909 and retained its title until shortly before the A's moved to Kansas City for the start of the 1955 season. The Phillies played their last game at the crumbling Baker Bowl on June 30, 1938, now co-existing with the A's at Shibe until that franchise relocated. Shibe Park itself was renamed Connie Mack Stadium prior to the 1953 season, and it was here the Phils became the sole occupant until its imminent demise claimed the last game in 1970.

As for National League Park, known and forever remembered as Baker Bowl, its legend among the old ballparks speaks for itself. For many it will be remembered as a landmark, perhaps a link from the 19th Century parks to the 20th Century stadiums. But for many baseball fans who find their connection to the game's history uninteresting, it ceases to exist. Baker Bowl, which was bordered by 15th, Huntingdon, Lehigh and Broad Streets in downtown Philadelphia, was demolished in 1950. To the casual observer, there is no trace of the magic of these games or the park they were played in.

~

WITHOUT A TRACE

The Phillies won the very first game played at Baker Bowl
But even on that April day, the park was getting old
A visible rise in center where the railroad ran so deep
The lawn required no mowers, as the stadium housed three sheep.

The Phils had bathed with Lifebuoy, but were loathe to stop the stink
The visitors often won the games, but what were they to think?
The park it seems fell awfully short, a vision not meant to be
Comforts built for the home team, were now sadly shared by Philly.

The right field line extended, some two-hundred and eighty feet
A forty foot wall was built, to keep balls from hitting Broad Street
So, how can you love a landmark, short of committing slander?
Lay it all on the shoulders of Grover Cleveland Alexander.

Grover Cleveland won ninety-four games in a span of three short years
In his prime, Chuck Klein starred here, and padded his storied career
The great Babe Ruth chose Baker Bowl to quietly leave the game
Forever linked, these three great men now grace the Hall of Fame.

The Phillies bid goodbye to the Bowl in 1938
The park had always felt like home but its time was running late
The writing on the proverbial wall, soon shifted the Phils to Shibe
Through Connie Mack's Athletics, flowed the ever-changing tide.

Baker's memories seem sad but sweet, some good, but rarely bad
Father Time pitched the last three outs, some say he always has
For the ghosts that haunt those hallowed streets, the park still has its place
For those who fail to remember, Baker's gone without a trace.

~ RWM

CHAPTER 5

~

FIRST TRIP

When I first landed at La Guardia Airport in Queens, New York, I knew no one. What the hell was I doing there? Believe me, that's another chapter altogether. I was supposed to meet someone at the airport but that scenario had completely slipped off the charts. I found myself in another world without a backup plan. As common sense and simple logic kicked in, I decided it was time to do what I do best. I sat in the airport lounge, had a few Buds and contemplated my next brilliant move. As much as I tried to ignore the obvious, it was time to come up with something resembling a plan. My vision was becoming far from clear but my thoughts were crystal.

I saw my very first New York City policeman and boldly chose to approach him. It was a wise decision. It would turn out to be an even greater first impression. I introduced myself (a dumb Canadian) and told him I had nowhere to go and no idea where I should be headed. My first time in New York City and I was in dire need of a little guidance. I asked if there was any area in the city that was not safe and should maybe be avoided. I could see the wheels turning as he looked from side to side and then focused back on me. "There's nowhere safe in New York City," was the unsettling reply. His response seemed a little jaded but I guess those words could be said about a lot of cities in North America. Or any continent for that matter. But at

29

this particular moment, that wasn't exactly the answer I was hoping to hear. He had confirmed my worst fears but did offer up a great tip that will stay with me forever. I still refer to it frequently and now share his wise words with anyone thinking of visiting New York City for the first time. "Try not to look like a tourist and walk around like you *own* the place." The clouds parted and tears came to my eyes. My new hero! I was literally hoping they were words to live by.

With that little jolt of adrenaline, I took a taxi to a much too expensive hotel across from the airport. I had no idea where I was or what my options might be. I checked in and made my way to the lounge and tried to pretend that I belonged here. Guess what? By the time I left the bar I had somehow convinced myself that I did belong. I own the place! The next morning I signed up for a tour of New York City and all its boroughs. I spent the day with a family from Delaware in a ten-seat minivan and had a blast! So much so that I resolved to take a bus from the Port Authority in Manhattan to Cooperstown in upstate New York the very next day. When will I ever get back here? Little did I know!

At the bus station they asked me if I wanted the Express bus or the milk run. I opted for the Express but was confused as the bus seemed to stop at any sign of life. It didn't matter where we were. If the driver saw someone standing on the highway with a couple of cabins in the distance, or if some mutt standing by the side of the road looked like he might want to hop on and sit a spell, we stopped! After a couple of hours the driver said we had a fifteen minute stop ahead if we wanted a coffee or maybe just stretch our legs. I saw him having a quick bite at the counter and decided to sit beside him.

"I thought this was an Express bus?" was my first question.

"It is," was the reply.

"But we've stopped at every standing structure and side street along the highway."

"How else do you expect these people to get around?"

I'm sure he didn't want to hear my solution. His answer canceled out my other questions and pretty soon we were back on our way. It was another long day but I was pleased with myself for not taking the milk run. I'd still be an hour and a half outside of Cooperstown. I understood what was he was saying but please! Could we just change the name from Express to, Hey, Need a Lift?

After a much too short day and a half in Cooperstown, I boarded the Trailways Bus back to the city. A few hours into a return bus ride that took me wide-eyed and smiling through small towns such as Oneonta, Delhi, New Platt, and Big Indian to name just a few, I came face to face with a startling discovery. I would be arriving at the Port Authority Bus Station very late into what was now becoming a very dark New York night (..."walk around like you own the place..."). As we approached the city, I chanced a quick glance at myself and realized that much to my chagrin, yes, I truly did look like a tourist. Literally, right off the bus. If my appearance didn't bring a serious bout of the giggles to any criminal upon sight, my travel bag would surely give me away and seal my fate. The cop at the airport would be so disappointed in me. Would they send my body home or would I be joining the lucky few who had now made the East River their permanent home? I practiced my best tough guy look and even rolled up my sleeves to show off my huge quivering biceps.

Upon arrival, I quickly found out where the bus to the airport and my hotel would be leaving from and tip toed into the sweat lodge my one hour wait for departure was soon to be. No sooner had I emerged on the street when the big city hit me. I tried so hard, but couldn't help but notice the three young men now approaching a young lady waiting for a local bus not too far from me. Like me, she seemed to be willing herself invisible. She was reading a magazine or at least pretending to, which seemed strange at the time as it was dark outside. Even with the street lights. They eyed her up and down, danced and teased all around her while one of them held a blaring ghetto blaster to his ear, creating some kind of primitive dance. They smiled and sang loudly to her face as I glanced around for the posse to ride in. A nightly ritual for these boys and maybe her as well but it didn't seem likely. Being true to my code of idiocy, I knew I'd eventually have to intervene. Here was a damsel in distress, but truth be told, at this particular moment I wasn't exactly in my comfort zone. Being out-numbered 3-1 caused a slight hesitation in my save-the-world act. Surprisingly, the young lady didn't seem to be bothered by all the attention. She was actually ignoring them with wondrous results! Another strange lesson learned in the big city. I will definitely mark that one down.

Thankfully and much to my surprise, the three of them finally tired of their own festivities and began to move along. I wasn't exactly young and pretty but I now wondered if their next target might just be yours truly. I can't stand ghetto blasters but hey, if push came to shove, I could surely learn to love the music they were playing! Could they sense that? Would I now be mistaken for a piñata dressed up as a Canadian tourist? But alas, they kept on going, seemingly oblivious now to anything and everything around them. I glanced down at my rolled up sleeves and exposed biceps one more time. My God, it worked!

I was now home free. Thirty more tense minutes until my ride was ready to leave. But just to be on the safe side, I approached the bus where my driver sat reading; biding his time, his head buried in a book until departure. Just another day for him I guess. I knocked softly on the door and when I finally got his attention, nose pressed firmly against the glass door, I feigned indifference and asked if I might wait in the safe confines of the bus. I'd like to believe he had witnessed the same scene as I had and perhaps understood my plight. Maybe it's just a replay witnessed by New Yorkers or residents of any big city night after night. He had a kind face and after much thought replied, "I shouldn't be doing this but hey, no problem." Thank you, sir, was smeared all over my face I'm sure of it. At last I could finally relax. At that point I figured drawing up my will could wait at least one more day.

My bus driver's name, I still remember to this day, was Archie. We had a wonderful conversation. I sat up front and as it turned out, I was his only passenger all the way to La Guardia. I couldn't believe, in a city this big, there were no passengers waiting anywhere. I had envisioned three-man teams with ghetto blasters waiting at each stop. All staring at my rolled up sleeves. Being Archie's only customer, he was able, and kind enough to drop me off right outside my hotel, against all rules. I believe he was from Jamaica originally, and if I remember correctly, was looking forward to his return home upon retirement. I sincerely hope he was able to reunite with his family and I wish him all the best. A good man for sure and I met quite a few on this trip. I knew I would sleep soundly once the key entered the lock of my hotel room and the next morning, I flew sadly away from one of my greatest adventures. Always to return! Five trips to the Hall of Fame and a dozen visits to New York City in the books and I can hardly wait for the next time I touch down.

~

On the topic of bus rides and trying to get around in New York City, I'd be remiss if I didn't give a tip of the hat to the taxi cabs. You really can't ignore them even if you tried. A sea of yellow greets your eyes every time you step outside. Occasionally you will see a few green cabs (which they call boro taxis, short for borough) but these operate only in restricted areas. If numbers interest you, there are approximately 13,000 taxis in New York City operated by well over 40,000 different drivers and provide transportation to roughly 240 million passengers per year. These men and women know the city and know what they are doing. They have made lane changes and pulling into traffic an art form. Controlled chaos! The traffic they create and maneuver around each day is mind boggling. Believe me, they are good at what they do and they have seen it all I'm sure. Strike up a conversation if you are adventurous or sit back and take in the sights. Most drivers will respond in a positive manner, some are real characters and talk your leg off but many of them would just rather go about their business. Don't get me wrong, they are polite, but if you're looking for small talk? Well, not so much.

As a small aside regarding taxis in New York City, I have to come clean about something I had always thought just couldn't be true. Before I had ever been to New York, the many movies and television shows I had watched always showed someone coming out of a hotel or a restaurant, onto the sidewalk and waving their hand in the air and bingo! Whad'ya know! A taxi was right there to deliver them safe and warm to their destination. Just more Hollywood crap is what I thought. Well, it's true! It doesn't seem to matter where you are in the city or what street you might find yourself on. A wave of the hand and a taxi is never far away. You might not be the only one running to grab the door handle but never fear, the taxi will be there. So conversely, if you find yourself in New York City and do not need a cab, whatever you do, don't stand on the street and raise your hand to point upward or take part in any waving or innocent gesture as three flashes of yellow will screech to a halt two feet from where you are standing. Okay, maybe a slight exaggeration but the point is, the streets are flooded with them.

They are an oasis in a rainstorm and a cool refuge from the summertime humidity of New York. For visitors, the only way to get around is walking, but unfortunately, if you don't walk or can't walk, you will miss so much. The decision to drive in the city is ultimately yours as well, but unless you really have to, it's not something anyone of sound mind wants to do. The transit system is truly the only way to get around and very dependable. Most of the time, taxis will deliver you to the exact spot you want to go but then again this is New York. Be prepared as anything goes!

I had been staying at the old Olcott Hotel (which is now unfortunately a private residence) on a trip to New York City in 1998. It was a fabulous location. Mere steps to Central Park and even closer to the Dakota Apartment building where a brilliant John Lennon had been shot on the sidewalk by a twisted gunman. A reminder that life can be fleeting and to live each day like you mean it. I had a wakeup call at 3:30 A.M. on the last morning of another New York holiday. I was booked for an early flight out of La Guardia and stepped into the street at 4:30 in the morning with little expectation of hailing a cab at that hour. I was on W. 72 between Columbus and Central Park West. It was still dark but no sooner had I raised my hand to flag a cab I saw floating down CPW than he was right there in front of me. I do love this city! I have no idea how he saw me, but I imagine they are trained to see five fingers in the air from a thousand yards. Night and day! So now when I watch a movie or TV show, and I see someone step out into the street and hail a cab I think, "What the hell took so long?"

I had three such rides to the airport at that time over a four-year period as the airline had the same departure time scheduled. It was a beautiful time in the morning. Looking back across the East River to the bright lights of Manhattan was a gift that will always be with me. On my first trip, I thought it was just pure luck in nabbing a cab but never did I have to wait for more than a few minutes at worst. Not bad for a dark side street in the middle of the night. The drivers were completely overjoyed when I told them where I was headed. As it turned out, none of them actually lived in Manhattan. It was just way too expensive. Most had homes and families in Queens so to grab a fare at that time meant they could just head home after dropping me off with a tidy sum on the meter and a healthy tip to boot. I'm sure there are drivers that live elsewhere but that was not my experience.

Striking up a conversation with a cab driver can sometimes be an informative discussion or an exercise in frustration. Put yourself in their shoes and take it from there. We are all just trying to make our way in this world. Taxi drivers mostly stick to a two-man schedule with each working a twelve-hour shift using the same cab. They begin and end their shifts between 4 and 5 A.M. and again twelve hours later. In the name of fairness, that means each driver will experience a morning or evening rush hour which of course means more fares. I have heard there can be as much as a 20 percent drop in available taxis around 5:00 in the morning and again at 5:00 or so in the evening due to the changeover. Most drivers have an infinite amount of patience on board as rush hour or any hour in New York City can be way over the top. Times ten! Stand on a busy street in Manhattan and count the number of horns honked in a minute. It's tough to keep up. Most of the drivers I encountered however were amiable, knowledgeable about their city, and willing to offer directions as well as opinions and advice. At times, unwanted.

On one occasion, we had just emerged from a Broadway musical around 4:30 in the afternoon and decided to have dinner at Tavern on the Green at W. 67 and Central Park West. On a less hectic day the taxi ride would have taken no more than ten minutes or so to go the twenty or more blocks we had to cover. A nice little walk on a better day but today we decided to give our feet a rest. We were lucky enough to grab a cab almost right away as a yellow taxi had just dropped someone off directly in front of us. "Where to folks?" We told him Tavern on The Green. 67 and Central Park West. "I know where it is! What I want to know is why do you want to go all the way up there?" I thought it was obvious. Dinner! "There are plenty of good places to eat around here." No kidding. There are literally thousands of them. We had decided on Tavern on The Green. "As you can see the traffic is going nowhere fast." Yes, I could see that. "Look folks, it's going to take me half an hour in this traffic to get there. You'd be faster to walk." We understood but weren't in the mood for walking so what was the problem? "I can take you there alright. But I can name you half a dozen restaurants right around the corner from here and they are all just as good as Tavern on the Green. Probably better!" This was the exercise in frustration. This went on for another minute or so but it became obvious we weren't going to get there in this cab. He seemed like a veteran of the car wars but today for some reason he didn't feel like getting involved. We had only traveled a block or so and the meter was barely past the starting point so we decided to cut our losses and bug out. I told him we would probably both feel better if we got out right here. "Have a nice day folks." And with that little discourse we poured out of the cab and went to look for a good little restaurant as he mentioned, right around the corner.

Speaking of transit, the first time or two trying to navigate your way around the New York City subway system can trigger a cause for alarm. You can't help but look around in desperation for someone to come a runnin', but never fear, help is never far away! (Depending on the hour). As much as you try to hide it, New Yorkers can spot a tourist a mile away. Just give in and ask someone. I guess it just seems that way now, but the maps, different colored letters and numbers that are designed to get you to your destination with supposed ease might as well have been in Swahili. The many stairwells, turnstiles, buskers and throngs of commuters can be dizzying. Just when you think you have found the right number, color, arrow or letter that leads you down the corridor or stairs to your train, don't pat yourself on the back just yet. You had better be facing the right way because the approaching train on the right will take you to the Promised Land but the one on the left will lead you far away in a real hurry. Panic can set in fast until you master the art of movement which is the Metro Transit Authority (MTA). Don't be shy. Really, just ask someone.

The great thing about the transit system in New York is that you can buy an MTA card for however long you need. One trip, a day, three days, a week, month, etc. and with one swipe you can hop on any subway or local bus any time you want for that duration. Believe me, it's a great way to get around. A little confidence wouldn't hurt either. Just remember that if you hop on the wrong bus or train, remember to hop off as well. If you make a mistake, roll with it. The next stop is only minutes away. Catch the next train going back the same way you came and try again. A small learning curve.

After my success with the cop at the airport I never once shied away from another policeman in New York. In some regards I came to think of them as not only my protectors in blue, but oddly enough, as travel consultants. They always came through for me. The security around the subway system and all of New York is extremely tight so you will always find someone with an NYPD or MTA patch on their shoulder. Walk on up to them and tell them I said it was okay. They are always looking for someone to talk to. I had one New York City policeman walk a whole block with me just to point out the closest bar. It was around the corner and up some stairs but he seemed to take a personal interest in my finding a cold beer. I invited him up but after a slight hesitation, he smiled and declined.

As I look back on my trips to the Big Apple, it turned out my worst fears about the city and the people who live there were completely unfounded. I now know for a fact that New Yorkers get a bad rap. I've heard them described as rude and arrogant amongst other things, but oddly enough, too many people reach these conclusions without ever setting foot in the city. Stereotypical crap! For the most part, the people mind their own business and they expect that you are doing the same. If I needed assistance, or a question answered, they never failed to answer the bell. To a person, they never let me down nor disappointed me. A helping hand should always be there no matter the city, but unfortunately that's not always the case!

But for the record, I love New York City! I always have and I always will. The people I met and talked with in my travels were not only approachable but accommodating and never failed to be hospitable. They were always willing to indulge me no matter how mundane the request. Take my word for it. New York City will pleasantly surprise you. It's a great place for people watching so look around; there is a lot to see. The city is full of characters but like any big city, be aware of your surroundings and don't get caught staring. Especially on the subway. If you have to, just roll up your sleeves and show them your biceps! Treat people the way you would want to be treated and guess what? Everyone's happy! I know I was! For years I thought of New York as just a far off land. Part of an enchanted fairy tale you see in the movies or read about in the newspapers. As is turns out, you can actually hop on a plane and fly there.

~

CHAPTER 6

~

OPENING DOORS

As a St. Louis Cardinal in the 1960s, Curt Flood excelled both on the field and off. His reputation as a fine ballplayer was indisputable. His numerous talents included more than just the tools of his sport. Curt Flood was one of the better ballplayers on a St. Louis club that fielded future Hall of Famers Orlando Cepeda and Bob Gibson, as well as Bill White and Roger Maris. As his career evolved, Flood was eventually named captain of the Cardinals and held that status from 1965 through 1969. In that five-year stretch, he led the St. Louis club to three pennants, before finally winning a World Series in 1967 against the Boston Red Sox. Off the field, he had many hobbies and not only owned his own photo shop but became a distinguished painter in his own right. Until her death in 2006, Coretta Scott King still had a portrait of her husband, Dr. Martin Luther King, Jr., painted by Flood, hanging in her residence. For many years, a picture which he had painted for St. Louis Cardinals and Budweiser owner, August A. Busch, Jr., was showcased on Busch's yacht. To complement his many gifts, Flood was an intelligent man and met with many influential people in his travels. A few of these acquaintances were to not only influence him, but raise his awareness of a changing world around him. Achieving greatness on the field would take a backseat to the historic and precedent setting events off the field for which his name will be forever linked.

Curtis Charles Flood, the last of six children, was born in Houston, Texas, January 18, 1938. He resided there for two short years before the family moved to a low-income neighborhood in Oakland, California. Despite constant reminders from friends and scouts alike regarding his 5 foot 7 inch, 140-pound stature, plus the fact he was a black man, his chances at a Major League career were a long shot at best. Regardless, Curt Flood was signed out of that Oakland ghetto by the Cincinnati organization in 1956 for the princely sum of $4,000.

Against all odds, Curt was able to silence his detractors in only his first year in the Red Legs Minor League system. He hit .340 with 29 home runs and was even rewarded with a short stint with the Major League club that same year. His first off-season experience gave him a taste of what the Major Leagues' reserve clause system was all about. It started him on a journey which was to eventually change the way clubs dealt with players' contracts, and changing the face of baseball forever!

Flood was both excited and hopeful that his first year's success would earn him a substantial increase at the negotiating table. Those wide eyes which harbored a ton of enthusiasm were now opened even further, as Cincinnati General Manager Gabe Paul explained the club's position. Paul's contention was that the clubs expenses were way out of hand and thought Flood should just renew the old agreement, take his promotion to a higher Minor League club, and continue to play hard. As had many of the players who found themselves in this exact same position before him, Flood had no alternatives but to accept. The reserve clause gave him no room for negotiations. "Baseball law" was how he described it. Looking forward to making a good impression and an improved fate for himself, Curt played hard and at year end, was met with the same proposal from management. Reluctantly, he re-signed once again, but shortly after, on December 5, 1957, he was traded to the St. Louis Cardinals. This trade worked in favor of Flood and enabled him to ignite the spark which carried the Cardinals to one of the most successful decades in team history. Curt was a loyal and dedicated player with his new organization and was a prominent figure off the field as well. He assisted in funding an organization which provided shoes to needy children in the St. Louis area called Aunts and Uncles.

After twelve successful years in St. Louis, Flood had found himself in his 30s, and the Cardinal organization had begun to look in a new direction. They had their sights set on a slugger named Dick Allen from Philadelphia, and Curt was made expendable. On October 7, 1969, the deal was completed, with St. Louis trading Flood, catcher Tim McCarver, Byron Browne and Joe Hoemer to the Phillies, for Allen, Cookie Rojas and Jerry Johnson. Curt was stunned. Twenty years later, while thinking back on his reaction to the trade, his comments were noted by filmmaker Ken Burns in his documentary "Baseball." "I'd often wondered what I would do if I were ever traded, because it happened many, many times. It was "part of the game," and then suddenly it happened to me. I was leaving probably one of the greatest organizations in the world at that time, for what was probably one of the least liked... by God, this is America. I'm a human being; I'm not a piece of property. I am not a consignment of goods."

The fact was, Flood was totally unaware of the deal that had been made, until a reporter called, looking for a response. The twelve years he had devoted to St. Louis caused him to become angry about the disrespectful way the trade had been handled, and also what he perceived to be harsh treatment towards black players in Philadelphia. Curt was quoted that he would "...be lying if I told you that as a black man in baseball, I hadn't gone through worse times than my teammates. I'll also say, yes, I think the change in black consciousness in recent years has made me more sensitive to injustice in every area of my life. But I want you to know that what I'm doing here, I'm doing as a ballplayer, a Major League ballplayer." On December 24, 1969, he sent a letter to then Commissioner of Baseball, Bowie Kuhn, which stated that he believed his rights as a citizen of the United States were in violation, and wished to obtain contract offers from teams other than Philadelphia. Flood publicly complained the trade "violated the logic and integrity of my existence..." He was denied by the Commissioner's Office.

Flood was an articulate and well-read man, and hungered for education as well as knowledge of the inequities in the world, in which, being a black man in America, he had experienced himself. In 1962, Curt was introduced to Johnny and Marian Jorgensen, two political activists from San Francisco who would greatly influence his life. Johnny was against violence, and before his own death in 1966, he made a vow to improve "his own corner of the planet with immaculate honor." This dedication so impressed Flood that after Johnny's death, he strove to serve his own principles as best he could. From his own book entitled "The Way It Is," he wrote, "Whatever I contributed to the unique morale of the Cardinals, was part of this growth, and so, of course, was my decision to have it out in public with the owners of organized baseball."

Curt believed the reserve clause denied the players the right to negotiate employment with teams of their own choosing. The Civil Rights Movement left Flood feeling, that as a black man and a professional ballplayer, he literally belonged to his team, like a piece of property. He now wanted to challenge this clause which baseball had established many years before, in the 1880s.

Not wishing to give into the trade, Flood finally decided to retire, but was given the idea of suing Major League Baseball, by his old friend, Marian Jorgensen. Flood thought the idea outlandish at first. The clause had been challenged by under the radar names such as Danny Gardella and George Toolson in the past, but never by a star with such a credible background in statistics and salary. Risking his $90,000 salary and possible future in the game, he decided to test "the invulnerability of baseball."

Bowie Kuhn had rejected Curt's claim of slavery, saying he didn't think of "its applicability to the situation at hand." Baseball had twice before, gone to the Supreme Court and was now headed for a third. Most fans and those involved in baseball couldn't believe that someone would risk such a high salary to pursue his own beliefs. Flood explained, "I'm a child of the 60s, I'm a man of the 60s. During that period of time, this country was coming apart at the seams. We were in Southeast Asia...Good men were dying for America and for the Constitution. In the southern part of the United States, we were marching for civil rights and Dr. King had been assassinated, and we lost the Kennedys. And to think that merely because I was a professional ballplayer, I could ignore what was going outside the walls of Busch Stadium [was] truly hypocrisy and now I found, that all those rights that these great Americans were dying for, I didn't have in my own profession."

In addition to an agreement to support him financially, the Major League Baseball Player's Association (MLBPA) and executive director Marvin Miller, warned Curt about endangering his baseball career and future earnings. After much personal deliberation, he decided the goal was worth the fight. He moved to Denmark to open a restaurant and pursue his other passion, which was painting. He sat out the 1970 season as the trial went to court, not wanting to prejudice the case against him. In August of that year, the Federal Court in New York had their answer. They ruled against Flood, citing the 1922 Supreme Court Decision that organized baseball was exempt from anti-trust laws because it was a sport. He appealed to the Supreme Court, but in a decision that finally arrived on June 12, 1972 he was, again, turned down. The Court ignored ex-Supreme Court judge, Arthur J. Goldberg, who was now one of the Flood's lawyers, and Flood himself, who claimed that the reserve clause violated anti-trust laws as well as the Thirteenth Amendment. Although it was a crushing defeat, the doors had now been opened for a legal attack on Major League Baseball.

Curt Flood took it hard, and the thrill and enthusiasm for playing the sport had left him. On November 3, 1970, the Phillies traded Flood once again to the Washington Senators. Reluctantly, he agreed to the deal, signing for $110,000, but his heart was just not in it. He played in thirteen games, but with only seven hits in thirty-five at bats, Curt Flood retired from baseball for good that April, and once again returned to Europe. He was proud that he had made sacrifices, by putting his own career and principles on the line, and stood up to the injustices of baseball that others before him had simply accepted.

Marvin Miller of the MLBPA now had a foot in the door and continued to fight for players' rights. Miller discovered a loophole in Major League Baseball contracts in 1975, stating that owners held the rights to players for only one year, after which the player could sell his services to the highest bidder. Baseball was once again on the ropes. A three-man arbitration board was set up to settle the position of both sides on this matter. The Board consisted of Miller, an MLB rep, and a labor negotiator named Peter Seitz. Even before the meetings, Seitz had made public the fact that he backed the union in this matter, and urged the owners to negotiate. But believing they were right the owners stood their ground. On December 23, 1975, Seitz, with the deciding vote, gave the decision to the players. The owners lost their appeal, and finally compromised with Miller to allow players to exercise their right to negotiate freely after six years of service. "Free Agency" was now the new baseball term. It was a symbolic precedent for a person's rights in general, for baseball and all sports as well. No longer would the owners or the Comiskeys of the baseball world throw its might and intimidation against what was now a powerful players union. In the end, they had Curt Flood to thank. He had finally seen his efforts come to fruition. Although it was too late for Curt himself to be monetarily affected by free agency, any player, present or future, would be well advised to throw some appreciation his way. He had stood up not only for his own principles, but for the future of professional ballplayers as well. Curt Flood will long be remembered and admired not only as an outstanding ballplayer, but as a fine human being.

He finished his career with a .293 batting average in 1,759 games, while collecting 1,861 hits and 7 Gold Gloves. A 1968 Sports Illustrated cover proclaimed him at that time, "The Best Center Fielder in Baseball," over players such as Willie Mays and Roberto Clemente. In 1967, he set a National League record for consecutive games in the outfield without an error at 227, including 568 chances.

Curt Flood died, ironically, on January 20, 1997, a day that was a celebration for the late Dr. Martin Luther King, Jr. He succumbed to throat cancer at the age of 59.

On the following page is a copy of the December 24, 1969 letter Curt Flood sent to Bowie Kuhn, stating his desire to play for other clubs in the upcoming 1970 baseball season.

~

December 24, 1969

Mr. Bowie K. Kuhn
Commissioner of Baseball
680 Fifth Avenue
New York, New York
10019

After twelve years in the Major Leagues, I
do not feel I am a piece of property to be
bought and sold irrespective of my wishes. I
believe that any system which produces that
result violates my basic rights as a citizen
and is inconsistent with the laws of the
United States and of the sovereign States.

It is my desire to play baseball in 1970,
and I am capable of playing. I have received
a contract offer from the Philadelphia Club,
but I believe I have the right to consider
offers from other clubs before making any
decisions. I, therefore, request that you
make known to all Major League Clubs my
feelings in this matter, and advise them
of my availability for the 1970 season.

Sincerely Yours,
Curt Flood

CURT FLOOD

Curt Flood died today
I don't know why I cried
I didn't even know the man
But it's deeper than that
Curt was one of them!

In a league of his own
He stood above them all
A man among men
At one time he stood tall
And put it all on the line
And then.......

He kicked down the doors
Threw open the gates
Surely, to him they owe
He opened their eyes
Hit 'em where it hurts!
Wouldn't we all like to be
A little more like Curt!

~ RWM

CHAPTER 7

~

HANK GREENBERG

Hall of Fame shortstop Honus Wagner once stated, "There ain't much to being a ballplayer, if you're a ballplayer." A simple statement made by a remarkable shortstop, but its implications run deep. Most ballplayers want to do exactly that. They want to play ball! Players would prefer not to be judged or critiqued (good luck) but instead be remembered by their exploits on the field rather than off. Unfortunately, history hasn't always honored that approach. Being a team player is very important in the makeup of a team especially if you want to win. Arrogance, work habits, attitude and lest we forget, the skills required to play the game are a few more reasons why some players make it and some don't. Unfortunately, in eras gone by, religion, race, color and ethnicity also played a major part and were key to a player's acceptance into the Major Leagues. Fortunately, over the years, many players pursued their dreams, and in doing so, overcame numerous obstacles, ultimately paving the way and opening doors for the many young men that would follow in their footsteps.

Jackie Robinson was perhaps the finest example of this pursuit, as no player before or after, endured such hatred and suffered through the continual barrage of racial taunts as he did. Through it all he somehow maintained a calm dignity and gentlemanly poise. He became the first black player to suit up for the Major Leagues, finally breaking in with the Brooklyn Dodgers in 1947. Regrettably, in the years leading up to this historic event, there were far too many ballplayers who, on a daily basis, endured the slurs and indignities as a result of their heritage, background or beliefs. Few suffered more abuse than the Jewish community.

On Sunday, August 29, 2004, the baseball Hall of Fame in Cooperstown, New York, sponsored a day entitled, A Celebration of Jews in Baseball. Attending the ceremony and representing the Jewish players were many former Major Leaguers including Elliot Maddox, who years before, adopted the Jewish religion as a young man. Also on hand were Norm Sherry, Mike Epstein, Ken Holtzman, Bob Tufts, Richie Scheinblum, and Ron Yellen. The last, but certainly not the least of the eight, was baseball's first designated hitter, Ron Blumberg, who recorded this milestone in 1973.

These proud men came from every corner of the USA to honor those of Jewish heritage who had played before, during, or after themselves. As well as laying a solid foundation for those in the game today, they set a clear path for the generations who would succeed them. Throughout the years, there has been a wealth of former and present players represented on Major League rosters and there will continue to be, far into the future.

One of the first Jewish players to take the field as a professional baseball player was Lipman "Lip" Pike, who played for the Troy Haymakers in 1871, the year the National Association founded the first pro league. Lipman Pike is not to be confused with another Jewish player of the same last name, Jacob Emanuel Pike, who suited up for Hartford of the National League in 1877. I'm sure we've all made that mistake.

Although they were reportedly the first to play, their fraternity remains a small percentage when you take into account the entire history of the game. Since 1871 to the present day, there have been roughly 18,000 players to play Major League Baseball, but somewhere in the neighborhood of 175 Jewish players, representing less than one percent of that total. Their numbers remain small but the impact they impressed on the game has been a long and lasting one! Of those roughly 175 players, a small number of them played in only one game, diminishing the figures somewhat. Taking that into consideration, from 1871 to 2002 they have accumulated over 2,000 home runs, while compiling a .265 batting average, (three percentage points higher than all other nationalities) with at least two players hitting for the cycle. Harry Danning accomplished the feat as a star catcher for the New York Giants in June of 1940 and in 2009, Ian Kinsler also hit for the cycle gathering hits in all six plate appearances. In April of 2011, Sam Fuld had already hit a home run, double and a triple needing just a single to reach this milestone as well. In the top of the ninth in Boston he hit a ball into left field and with his team screaming at him to stop at first, he instead rounded the bag and made it safely into second showing his integrity for the game and not just personal statistics.

Jewish pitchers have garnered a 3.66 ERA between the years of 1871 to 2002, a touch better than the 3.77 total for all other pitchers combined. Only two have thrown no-hitters, but Sandy Koufax has thrown four himself, (including a perfect game) and longtime Oakland Athletics pitcher Ken Holtzman has two to his credit. Legend has it, that longtime former Major League catcher and WWII spy Moe Berg, has the only baseball card displayed in the offices of the CIA. You can read all about the life of Berg in the book documenting his life, entitled, "The Catcher was a Spy" by Nicholas Dawidoff. The scholarly Berg was a fine defensive catcher but hit only .243, with a mere six home runs to show for his years in the sport. The stock phrase heard many times over the years, with its humorous tone, apparently sums up the career of Moe Berg, states, "he could speak a dozen languages but couldn't hit in any of them." At a hospital in Newark, New Jersey some years ago, a nurse at his bedside recalled Berg's final words before he passed away. "How did the Mets do today?" A baseball fan to the end!

A few years ago at a Sunday afternoon fundraiser, the American Jewish Historical Society, in co-operation with Jewish Major Leaguers Inc., teamed up in issuing a commemorative baseball card set entitled Jewish Major Leaguers: American Jews in America's Game. The limited edition set contains 141 cards, listing every identifiable player from 1871 to the 2003 All-Star break, including 42 players who will finally receive their first and only publicly issued card. A fitting tribute for the Jewish ballplayers, pioneers and trailblazers!

Perhaps Hall of Fame President Dale Petroskey summed it up best in this welcoming statement on the aforementioned Sunday in August. On the steps of the Hall of Fame building, during the opening ceremony for the Celebration of Jews in Baseball day, he remarked "...Is there any other sport like ours that allows us to blend our customs and our beliefs and our culture with our passion for the game? It's a beautiful thing." Indeed it is!

No list of luminaries could be considered complete, without honoring one of the games' finer human beings, a man who became not only an icon for his religion, but an enduring legend for baseball and all sports. During a war-shortened career, Hank Greenberg accumulated staggering statistics in only 9½ interrupted Major League seasons.

In Peter Lavine's book entitled, "Ellis Island to Ebbetts Field," a Walter Matthau quote summed up Greenberg's exalted status this way: "You couldn't help but be exhilarated by the sight of one of our own guys looking like Colossus."

Henry Benjamin Greenberg was born in Manhattan's Lower East Side on New Year's Day, January 1, 1911. Born to parents David and Sarah Greenberg, both recent Romanian immigrants, the young Greenberg moved with his family to the Bronx at the age of six and remained there for the remainder of his childhood. He attended the borough's Hebrew schools and found himself playing baseball in his spare time, mostly because all his friends were enjoying America's favorite past-time. He didn't want to be left out. His size, and desire to excel in everything he pursued, would lead him down a path to not only a Major League career, but eventual, and eternal stardom. He was idolized by baseball fans and the growing Jewish community, and was looked upon as a fine example for followers of any religion. As one observer would later note, Greenberg's accomplishments both on and off the field did help the Jewish community's status by "...showing we were as American as everybody else."

Hank soon grew to love the game and became a New York Giants fan, following the team's exploits in the now fabled Polo Grounds. His parents had high hopes for their son, but could hardly envision Greenberg's own aspirations of making the sport, not only a career, but a dream for the future. During an interview in 1935, while playing for the Detroit Tigers, he explained his predicament to a reporter from the Detroit Jewish Chronicle this way: "Jewish women on my block...would point me out as a good-for-nothing, a loafer and a bum who always wanted to play baseball rather than go to school. Friends and relatives sympathized with my mother because she was the parent of a big gawk who cared more for baseball...than schoolbooks. I was Mrs. Greenberg's disgrace." His parents were somewhat distraught with the ongoing situation. The love they had for their son stood far above all else and they soon came to not only understand and accept his decision, but strongly support his desire for the game that had become such an immense part of who he was.

At the tender age of nineteen, Hank was not only turning numerous heads his way, but because of his raw talent, work ethic, and 6 foot 4 inch frame, caught the attention of four Major League teams. He was eventually scouted by his favorite Giants, but at the time, New York manager John McGraw, simply implied he didn't think Hank would make a Major League ballplayer. The Washington Senators had a fine first baseman by the name of Joe Judge and decided to abandon their interests and head in another direction. The New York Yankees had a kid by the name of Lou Gehrig and, (although they did make him an offer) for obvious reasons, neglected to pursue Greenberg any further. That left the Detroit Tigers, who were delighted to sign him for a mere $9,000. To satisfy his father's wishes, his contract called for him to earn a college degree before reporting to the Major League club. Hank's passion for the game became an obstacle to his studies, and by the end of his first year at New York University, he decided to devote all his time to the pursuit of a baseball career. He left school in 1930, and after three years in the minors, playing in towns such as Beaumont, Texas, finally joined the Detroit Tigers in 1933.

He was to play first base in "Bengaltown" for seven years before eventually moving to the outfield to make way for a young and a talented ballplayer by the name of Rudy York. Hank was more than gracious when asked to make the switch, believing that the move could only make the team stronger. Hank had always been a winner and was fortunate throughout his career to be surrounded by such high caliber teammates as Mickey Cochrane, Billy Rogel, Goose Goslin, Hal Newhouser and Charlie Gehringer.

The game of baseball has always enjoyed an abundance of colorful nicknames which help us to identify many of our favorite players, even to this day. Greenberg's Tigers were no different, sporting names like Schoolboy Rowe, Dizzy Trout, Chief Hogsett, Preacher Roe, Bucky Harris and Jo Jo White. Hammerin' Hank Greenberg was a standout even among those elite peers. By the time he retired after the 1947 season, he had amassed 331 home runs and 1,276 RBI, while batting .313. A high average for a slugger of his stature.

51

As previously mentioned, Hank gave up almost four prime years to the war effort. Many experts agree, that if he had played those years and remained healthy, his home run totals could have arguably reached well over 500, with a RBI projection closing in on 2,000. In his 9½ seasons, he played in four World Series, winning two. The first one came in 1935 and the other in 1945, both, ironically, against the hard-luck Chicago Cubs. He was also the first ballplayer to win an MVP at two different positions; in 1935 at first base, and in 1940, after switching to left field. He was elected to appear in four All-Star games, and ended his regular season career with a .605 slugging percentage and an on-base percentage of .412. An amazing compilation of figures.

Throughout Greenberg's illustrious career, numerous events occurred which helped to shape the man and the ballplayer. The most famous of these came in 1934, with his refusal to play in a game on Yom Kippur. This is one of the Jewish peoples' most important days, when all the sins of the past year are "wiped away" through fasting and prayer. It was a difficult decision for Hank as he was admittedly, not a particularly devout person, but eventually decided to sit the game out, respecting his father's wishes, who some say "put his foot down."

Detroit lost 5-2 to the Yankees that day, but upon his arrival at the synagogue, Greenberg was startled to receive a standing ovation from the huddled masses. Doubtless to say, he was red faced, but at that moment he came to realize what he meant to so many as a Jewish hero. In Hank's own words, "It's a strange thing when I was playing; I used to resent being singled out as a Jewish ballplayer. I wanted to be known as a great ballplayer, period. I'm not sure why or when I changed because I'm still not a particularly religious person. Lately though, I find myself wanting to be remembered not only as a great ballplayer but even more as a great Jewish ballplayer." As much as Hank had now realized his true worth, he acknowledged that he meant much more as a representative of his people, not only as Jews, but as Americans!

Edgar Guest immortalized the occasion with his tribute poem to Hank Greenberg entitled "Come Yom Kippur":

Come Yom Kippur – holy fast day worldwide over to the Jew
And Hank Greenberg to his teaching and old tradition true

Spent the day among his people and he didn't come to play
Said Murphy to Mulroney; "We shall lose the game today!
We shall miss him on the infield and shall miss him at the bat
But he's true to his religion – and I honor him for that."

For the most part, as Jackie Robinson later experienced, Hank silently endured endless discrimination and racial torments. It bothered him, to say the least, but he was proud of his heritage and was determined to struggle through. Teammate Birdie Tebbetts once suggested Hank was the most abused player in history outside of Robinson. Greenberg himself exclaimed, "As soon as you struck out, you weren't only a bum, you were a Jewish bum." Years later, Tebbetts, along with then Yankees Executive Vice President Arthur Richman, and legendary Hall of Famer Ted Williams, remembered the day Greenberg challenged the entire White Sox team after suffering taunts directed at him all day long. Hank yelled out to the opposing dugout, "If you got a gut in your body, you'll stand up!" As Williams recalled, "You know who stood up? Nobody!"

Suffice it to say, Greenberg more than persevered. In 1937, he fell one RBI short of Lou Gehrig's American League record of 184, and in 1938, he came within two home runs of the immortal Babe Ruth's record of 60 for a season. He reached 58 with five games remaining in the schedule, but many believe there were very few players who wanted a Jew to break the Babe's record, and accordingly, refused to give him any pitches to hit.

Hank remained a class individual throughout and never once complained or even spoke of these allegations, which in all likelihood, were true. Nonetheless, his 58 home runs that year, tied future Hall of Famer Jimmy Foxx's total for most homers by a right-handed batter. A record which lasted for 60 years until 1998 when Mark McGwire and Sammy Sosa surpassed them both. This new record remains tainted in my opinion as recent developments involving the use of steroids have suggested.

In 1941, after the Japanese bombed Pearl Harbor and America joined the war, Hank became the first American League player to enlist. He joined the Army Air Corps and rose to the rank of Captain, commanding a B-29 bomber squadron in the China-Burma-India theater, before coming back a war hero in September, 1945.

After missing three full seasons and parts of two others, he rejoined his Tiger club fresh out of the military and connected for a home run in his first game back. Detroit was in a tight pennant race in 1945, and at the end of that month needed one more win to clinch the American League banner. It was in the last regular season weekend of that historic year that Hank hit perhaps the most famous home run of his storied career. Down 3-2 in the top of the ninth inning, to the St. Louis Cardinals, Greenberg's grand-slam vaulted the Tigers into the Playoffs once again. He won his second World Series in four tries that same year and unbeknownst to him at the time, played only one more year in Detroit. The following year, 1946, his first full season after returning home from the Army, he led the AL with an incredible 44 home runs and 127 RBI. We are resigned to mere speculation as to what his statistics might have been, had he played during those war years.

Hank could feel the years taking their toll and knew, as the Tigers also did, that the end of his playing career was fast approaching. Detroit sold him to the Pittsburgh Pirates in 1947, which would turn out to be his last year of professional baseball. His arrival in Pittsburgh was widely anticipated and the Pirates rewarded Hank by making him the first player in history to reach the $100,000 mark in salary. They even renamed the left field bleachers Greenberg Gardens, and waited for the home runs to fly over the wall. His knees were slowly giving out as he approached his 37th birthday, but still managed to hit 25 round-trippers. It was while he was in Pittsburgh that he was able to play one year with a kid named Ralph Kiner. It was just like Greenberg to take him under his wing. It's no surprise Kiner himself would later enter the hallowed halls of Cooperstown. Hank's one year in the National League also brought him in close contact with a young man named Jackie Robinson. After an accidental collision at first base, as fate would have it, Robinson and Greenberg secured a lasting friendship between them. Jackie would later praise Hank as a class gentleman saying, "It sticks out all over Greenberg."

In his first year of retirement from playing a game that would grant him lasting immortality, Bill Veeck and the Cleveland Indians hired Hank as a baseball executive. He continued his legendary status by helping the Indians win pennants in 1948 and 1954, while setting attendance records along the way. Perhaps in part, because of his own close ties to Robinson, and remembering his own fight for acceptance, Hank became a major force in helping lead the campaign to integrate black players into baseball.

In 1958, he followed Veeck to the Chicago White Sox as a part owner and Vice President, and in 1959, helped the Sox to their first pennant in 40 years. He left the White Sox in 1961 to move to New York. There, he became an investment banker before moving on to Beverly Hills, making himself at that time, one of baseball's most successful ex-players.

Hank Greenberg will always be remembered for his achievements not only on the field, but for his well-respected stature off the field as well. He was the first player that we know of to ever give a party for the grounds crew. On the Detroit Tigers' off days, the groundskeepers knew not to put the tarp on the field as it was said that Hank would always pay a half dozen kids $20 a piece to shag balls for him. He used to walk along Michigan Avenue on his way to ballgames and would often wave and stop to talk to people along his route. He answered many of his letters personally, and in one particular leap year, 1936, a 13-year-old girl wrote to Greenberg proposing marriage to him, citing an aged custom. Hank responded apologetically in a hand written letter, saying he wasn't quite ready to marry at that time. Around 1938, as a community relations event, the Tigers paid for the United Hebrew schools to come to Briggs Stadium to see a game. With the game unfolding, one boy, as a joke, called out to Hank in Yiddish saying he was hungry. Greenberg turned and called to a peanut vendor, telling him to give the kid a box of peanuts and charge it to him. That was Hank!

Years later, Greenberg became one of the first players to charge for autographs advising his fans that checks were to be made out to his favorite charity, "Pets Adoption." Hank then matched every dollar, paying it out of his own pocket. In 1970, Hank testified for Curt Flood in his fight to dissolve the reserve clause in baseball. Again he was on the side of right, as the clause was eventually abolished by Major League Baseball in 1975. Players today still enjoy the benefits and freedom of choice their predecessors struggled so hard to obtain.

After sitting out Yom Kippur in 1934, the holiest day of the Jewish calendar, Bud Shaver of the Detroit Times wrote, "His fine intelligence, independence of thought, courage and his driving ambition have won him the respect and admiration of his teammates, baseball writers and the fans at large. He feels and acknowledges his responsibility as a representative of the Jews in the field of a great national sport, and the Jewish people could have no finer representative." There is no need to add to this deserving and appropriate tribute.

In 1983, the Detroit Tigers held a special ceremony to retire Greenberg's uniform, number 5, and at the same time, retired long-time friend and teammate Charlie Gehringer's number 2. A fitting remembrance for Hank Greenberg, a man that no less than Joe DiMaggio once called," one of the truly great hitters."

Three years later, on September 4, 1986, after a thirteen-month struggle with cancer, Hank Greenberg passed away at the age of 75, in Beverly Hills, California. His remains are entombed at Hillside Memorial Park Cemetery in Culver City. Surely, it's an understatement to say, we shall never see his like again.

~

The Life and Times of Hank Greenberg, a documentary by Aviva Kempner, has won many critics association awards and is available for fans wishing more information on this baseball legend. Shortly before his death, Hank paired himself with author Ira Berkow to write his autobiography entitled "Hank Greenberg – The Story of My Life."

CLASS TELLS

In 1911 on New Years Day, baseball had a new beginning
Into the world he was born to play, and would prove it inning after inning.
Raised in the Bronx as a Giants fan, he played because all the boys did
At 6 foot 4, he was a giant of a man, but in his heart he remained a kid.

Everyone knew him as "Hammerin' Hank", he ascended to tame "Bengaltown"
As a model he had Lou Gehrig to thank, in the mirror he laid his swing down
A family man who was raised on right, cut off from Detroit and Briggs
He often stayed home on Saturday nights, even after making the "Bigs."

A standout, surrounded by legends, a career full of hits and home runs
Gehringer, Cochrane and Goslin, couldn't match his 331.
In '38, 58 homers came close, but 60 belonged to the Babe
The record in sight with five games to go, New York is where it would stay.

They called him the "baseball Moses", a Biblical name but it's true
He came up smelling like roses, a gentleman clean through and through.
One Sunday he chose to sit himself down, to celebrate Yom Kippur
A man of his word and religion, very few knew what he endured.

Jackie shone like a magic wand; soared above his own private hell
The two had formed an incredible bond, about Hank he remarked, "Class tells."
"It sticks out all over Greenberg," this after a chance collision
It was only pitchers Hank wanted to hurt, RBI were his passion and vision.

He was shipped overseas, the first to enlist, his integrity fully intact
Four long years, his bat surely missed, the man homered his first game back
He made the Hall in '56, a shoe-in beyond any queries
One of Cooperstown's favorite picks, two MVPs and two World Series.

Edgar Guest had praised him in prose, Curt Flood will always remember
Above most men he continually arose, until that day in September.
The fourth of the month in '86, Hank Greenberg suddenly died
By baseball and family, forever missed; Heaven's gift was big number 5.

~ RWM

CHAPTER 8

~

YOU NEVER KNOW

I think it is safe to say that any team ever assembled has at least one player who believes they are far better than their coaches perceive them to be. At the end of the day, that very player will spend far too many games as a spectator gathering stale memories as well as a few well-placed splinters debating that very point. Getting into the game after all, is what it's all about. To finally get the chance to prove yourself! To reveal your true worth to the waiting baseball world. The great Dwight D. Eisenhower once reflected in a rare, fragile moment, "Not making the baseball team at West Point was one of the greatest disappointments of my life, maybe my greatest." As Ike so selflessly announced, many of us will go to great lengths and endure countless sacrifices in the never-ending quest for success *in* the game, and *for* the game. When personal goals are not met, through no fault of our own, of course, we are left with what *could* have been, or perhaps, in our own minds, what *should* have been.

The game itself is so unbelievably unpredictable. You never know what to expect on any day when you show up at the ballpark. In a game a few years ago, I remember stepping into the batter's box facing the fact that the previous six players had somehow gotten base hits just before me. The game was now well in hand but a tiny bit of pressure still pressed on me. I somehow singled to center to drive in another run but as the baseball gods would have it, we were no-hit in a game shortly after. Just when we thought we had it all figured out we were slapped back into reality! That's baseball for you; always back to the drawing board.

I recall an annual fastball tournament we had entered that our team had participated in a few times over the years. We were still spirited lads in our wide-eyed twenties looking for a game and a good time. On a Friday afternoon, after the long work-week was over, we drove to Salmon Arm from Vancouver, some five hours away, for our first game and an 8:30 Saturday morning start. Being young and full of piss and vinegar, we arrived late in the evening and proceeded to partake in the social activities that precluded any baseball weekend. It wasn't just the game itself, as I've earlier indicated, but an acquired taste for the sport and all it has to offer.

As we drank into the small hours of the morning, someone interrupted the revelry to remind us of a game we had come to play in. Oh yeah! The first pitch was now roughly six hours away. As game-time approached, our collection of misfits, complete with blood-red eyes, four hours of sleep and pounding heads, souvenirs of the previous night's accomplishments, began to wander into the park from all directions. It was a cold and drizzly morning and the pre-game warm-up, with its sawdust sprinkled field, had hardly brought us anywhere close to warm or warmed up. We were, incidentally, a very good team, but failed to prove ourselves for the first six innings.

As the seventh and final inning presented itself, we found ourselves on the wrong side of a 7-3 score. In our last at bat, a few of the cobwebs had mysteriously disappeared. We managed to accumulate a few base runners and had even scored a couple of runs. Most of us, at this stage of the game, were half-expecting to lose this first contest. Collectively, we would have been mildly content with a 7-5 loss, proud of our gallant last ditch effort, knowing that at least this setback would have awarded us a 4:30 afternoon game. That pleasant thought included a much-needed chance to nurse our heads, grab a few winks, chow down and prepare ourselves for the reality, and uncertainty of a long and winding road up the tournament ladder. A difficult, but attainable back door journey. But as we all know, it's not over 'til it's over! As fate would have it, our shortstop and slugger came to the plate with two on and two out and promptly hit a 3 run shot for an 8-7 win. Our unlikely reward was now a one hour reprieve before our next game.

A game which had now put us into the winner's bracket, and a much too soon 11:00 A.M. start. I have to this day, never seen such sad faces on a winning team in my life. Talk about a deer in the headlights. You'd have thought someone had just shot the team mascot. Moments earlier, we had begrudgingly anticipated the loss. A chance to soothe our wounds with the welcome assistance of a five-hour recuperation period. We now had one hour to gobble hotdogs and aspirin and get ready for our next well-rested opponent. After the initial surprise of a shocking and unexpected win sunk in, our hero endured the running of the gauntlet and some good-natured ribbing. We all laughed ourselves into the future and collectively awaited the outcome of the next game.

Momentum can be a strange beast, and by the time the long weekend Monday had arrived, we found ourselves in a semi-final game against the team from Wenatchee, Washington. This was a team that had not only traveled twice as far as we had to compete, but seemed to be having at least as much fun as we were having. If not more! The long distance required and time involved for the travel itself had resulted in a lineup that boasted the bare minimum of nine Wenatchee players. A skeleton of a team, at best. They could scarcely afford to lose anyone, but as events sometimes shake out, one of their players went down with an ankle injury in a gutsy win prior to our upcoming showdown. As expected, and with no real alternatives, they toughed it out and took to the field with a team of eight tired but more than willing players. Well, wouldn't you know it! With only two outfielders, they beat us! They deserved full marks for their victory! They were a great bunch of guys and with stellar pitching and timely hitting, they beat us 4-0. They more than deserved the win.

As a result of us losing the third place game, we decided to cheer for the Wenatchee team in the tournament's final game against the obviously favored home team from Salmon Arm. Again, obviously playing a man short, they seemed to be a sentimental favorite, even amongst a surprising portion of the hometown faithful. They were battling with a boatload of heart but down a couple of runs in the third inning, when our first baseman decided he was going to boost their confidence and lead us in a resounding cheer. Beer gardens can be a wonderful thing. Every one of us to a man assured him of our loyal backing, and with that he bounded down the stadium stairs, positioned himself front and center and steadied himself. Ready to rally us in a show of support with a, "Give us a W" cheer. The W, of course, being the first of the all too many letters, ultimately spelling out Wenatchee. After bounding down the stairs, hoping to inflict an influence on the outcome of the game, ultimately baring his soul in front of the few hundred fans gathered for the final, we all huddled in agreement and decided to remain silent as he tried in vain to coax a cheer out of us. As the first unsettling moments of silence greeted him with his first plea of "Gimme a W" hanging in the air, you would have thought he'd seen a ghost. After a sobering blank stare and a few moments of solitude, he begged of us, "C'mon you guys, gimme a W!" Our team and the entire stadium felt for him but couldn't hold back the laughter. The tears were streaming down our faces. It didn't take him long to abandon his position or his good intentions and struggle back up the bleacher steps, his pride dragging far behind him. After more than a few expected curses, he broke down, still red faced, and laughed along with the rest of us. You gotta love this game! As it turned out, the Washington team could have used the cheer. Although they were ironically shutout 4-0 as we had been, they had gained an unwavering allegiance of fans, but unfortunately, as fate would have it, only a second place finish. Not surprisingly, no one on our team ever again volunteered to lead us in a cheer.

The boys looking respectable for a change.
(Courtesy of AAA Sports Photography)

~

CHAPTER 9

~

EBBETS FIELD

To many Brooklyn Dodger fans, Ebbet's Field was a cathedral and the home team became their only religion. Since the very first game played at the park on April 9, 1913, the people of Brooklyn took to the team like a long lost brother. The Dodgers called Brooklyn home from the year of their inception in 1884, with attendance that first year reaching a meager 65,000. At the time, they belonged to the American Association of baseball and stayed until 1889, before finally introducing themselves to the National League in 1890. One hundred and thirty years later the team still remains in that very same league. Unfortunately, what has changed is the city and the beloved park in which they played in.

Charles H. Ebbets gained sole ownership of the Brooklyn franchise in 1898 and held that title until his death in 1925. It became glaringly obvious to Ebbets early on that his passion for the game and the team he loved was rabidly infectious. The growing legions of fans that attended games at their present home of Washington Park were a testament to that fact. The park was far from the vision the new owner had in mind for his team, so Ebbets embarked on a plan to construct a park that would not only meet the needs of an ever increasing fan base, but give the New York borough a home to be proud of, complete with a wish list of memories that would continue through the ages. Ebbets Field was constructed on an old garbage dump appropriately named Pigtown at a cost of $750,000. In its day, the park was indeed the talk of the town, if not all of baseball. Their previous home, Washington Park, was located near the Gowanus Canal on Third Street and Fourth Avenue in the Red Hook section of Brooklyn. The Dodgers called this park home from 1898 to 1912, a span of a mere fourteen years. With the following year came the move to Ebbets Field and from there they formed a lasting relationship with the surrounding community. A relationship that survived four and one half decades until the unfortunate events of 1957.

Upon entering this brilliant new centerpiece, visitors to the park were greeted with nothing less than an 80-foot rotunda with decorated floors made of imported Italian marble. The bold pattern emblazoned on the marble replicated the stitching like that found on a Major League baseball. If fans were to gaze skyward they would have found themselves gaping in awe at a sizeable, marvelously crafted chandelier with twelve arms extending from it in the shape of, what else, but baseball bats. From these arms, or bats, hung twelve globules shaped like, you guessed it– baseballs. The entranceway crossed the corners of Sullivan Place and McKeever Place, and from that main gate Sullivan and McKeever ran parallel to the right and left field lines respectively. Montgomery Street ran from left field to center field, leaving the cobblestone-tiled Bedford Avenue to connect right field to center. The most loyal baseball fans and historians still consider this site and its boundaries a sanctuary. The move west from Red Hook to the new stadium in Flatbush, further established an enduring bond between the Brooklyn players and the neverending trail of paying customers.

Charles Ebbets had his own idea of the park's place in history and together with his passion and knowledge for America's favorite game, placed the Brooklyn Dodgers on a pedestal. For the most part, they made themselves and the franchise itself the envy of all their peers. Ebbets' love for the game was contagious and he spoke of his team and the sport in an almost spiritual sense. He once articulated, "Man may penetrate the outer reaches of the universe, he may solve the very secret of eternity itself, but for me, the ultimate human experience is to witness the flawless execution of a hit and run." Impressive!

When Ebbets Field opened in 1913, the seating capacity was a mere 25,000, with ballpark dimensions reaching 419 feet in left field, if measured from home plate, extending to 477 feet in center, and a paltry 301 feet down the right field line. The only covered portions of the park ran from an area past third base, circling back around home plate, all the way down to the foul pole in right. In the 1920s and right through to the 1932 season, Ebbets Field continued to add extra covered seating until the capacity reached 32,000, ultimately changing the park's distances to all fields. By the time the early 1940s arrived, the field had at long last been stabilized, making it 348 feet to the left field wall, 389 feet to dead center, and an even shorter 297 feet to right field. All left-handed hitters gave thanks to the powers that be! The power alleys were set at approximately 365 to left center and only 315 to right center. Ebbets Field had transformed itself from a pitcher's park to a hitter's park, and the ensuing results enabled power hitters such as Duke Snider to consider Ebbets Field a dream come true! Years later with Walter O'Malley as its new owner, the franchise shifted to Los Angeles, breaking many a Brooklyn heart and Snider is said to have broken down and cried. In Snider's own words, "We wept, Brooklyn was a lovely place to hit. If you got a ball in the air, you had a chance to get it out. When they tore down Ebbets Field, they tore down a little piece of me!" Many of the Dodger faithful shed tears right alongside their hero, and the heartbreak continues to this day.

As successful as the 1940s edition of the Brooklyn Dodgers were, the '20s and '30s were not always so kind. A single, somewhat embarrassing event that took place on the field on August 15, 1926, perhaps epitomized an era best forgotten, if not for the humorous tone it carried for some years. With the visiting Boston Braves in town, the bottom of the seventh inning arrived with Brooklyn and the Braves tied, with one out, and the bases full of Dodgers. Babe Herman, a hometown favorite, approached the plate with Chick Fewster on first, pitcher Dazzy Vance on second and the team's catcher on third. Herman hammered a long fly ball to right field, and Vance not knowing whether the ball would be caught or not, moved cautiously away from second base. When the ball hit the right field wall, Vance made his way around third base and somewhat beyond. The catcher originally on third scored easily but because Dazzy was so slow in reacting, he only made it halfway down the third baseline before having second thoughts and, initiating his retreat, returned to the base. Fewster, who had seen the play developing in front of him, thought he could trot easily into third base, which he did, just as Vance slid back into that very same bag.

Now let's not forget about Babe Herman. Herman himself obviously never forgot the play nor lived it down for the rest of his life. Years later, Herman recalled the disaster in his own words: "I saw the ball hit the wall as I was on my way to first base and from the way it bounced, I figured I could make it to second. I slid into second safely with a double, but as I'm lying down I see that a rundown is taking place between third and home. Naturally, I figure it is Chick Fewster in the rundown, who'd been on first, so I get up and sprint for third like I'm supposed to, that way we'll have a man on third base even if Fewster is tagged out.

"But when I get to third, Fewster is *already* there, which surprises me. And here comes Vance into third from the other side. That *really* surprises me, 'cause I thought he'd scored long ago. After all, he was on second and even if you're slow as a turtle you should be able to score from second on a double.

"Anyway, there we are, all three of us on third base at one and the same time. The Boston third baseman, Eddie Taylor, doesn't know what to do, so he tags all of us. Vance was declared safe and Fewster and I were both out. If there was any justice, Vance would have been the one declared out, because he's the one caused the traffic jam in the first place. But down through history, for some strange reason, it's all been blamed on me." It wasn't uncommon for the team, even many years after the play, to be referred to as the "three men on third" team for obvious reasons. As folklore would have it, the incidents and its details outgrew reality. Fans and players from around the league began to think Babe Herman had tripled into a triple play. But the Braves had already recorded one out in the inning, so this scenario was impossible. John Lardner perhaps trying to dispel the rumors, wrote in his newspaper article, "Babe Herman never tripled into a triple play, but he did double into a double play which is the next best thing."

As time went by, a story somehow trickled down through the years, and whether authentic or not, managed to sum up a tongue-in-cheek image it took the Dodgers some time to overcome. Years later, as the story goes, one of Brooklyn's many taxicabs was making its way to a fare when the driver edged past Ebbets Field, rolled down his window and yelled up to a spectator in the nearby grandstand. "How's the game going?" The fan, oblivious to the irony of his answer, called back "The Dodgers have three men on base!" "Ah," the cabdriver said, "which base?"

There were better things to come for "The Boys of Summer" as Roger Kahn called them in his 1972 book of the same name. This baseball classic covered the Brooklyn Dodgers as recalled from Kahn's own childhood, his two years (1952 and 1953) covering the team for the New York Herald Tribune, and subsequent interviews with the Brooklyn players some 20 years later. This book has stood the test of time and is a terrific read.

The Brooklyn Dodgers finally won their first and only World Series title in 1955 after seven previous losses in the Fall Classic. The last five setbacks came at the sure hands of their crosstown rivals, Casey Stengel's New York Yankees. They eventually took the Series from those same Yankees winning the seventh and deciding game 2-0 behind the brilliant pitching of Johnny Podres. Future Hall of Famers Jackie Robinson, Dizzy Dean, Duke Snider, Pee Wee Reese, and Roy Campanella, as well as favorites Carl Furillo, Gil Hodges, and many other home town heroes were all part of the magic that was the Brooklyn Dodgers. They truly touched the hearts of all Brooklyn residents and managed to bring all races together with one common bond. Baseball!

Ebbets Field itself witnessed many historical events including the afore-mentioned eight World Series appearances. Some memories were not quite as glamorous as others. For example, the introduction of yellow baseballs was an experiment the League initiated, hoping to make the ball easier to see. This game took place between the Dodgers and Cardinals on August 2, 1938, but immediately flopped as neither the players or the fans took to this odd change in their beloved game. Major League Baseball televised its very first game at Ebbets Field one year later on August 26, 1939, with coverage of the first game of a double header between the Dodgers and Cincinnati. This milestone was a huge success, and the following day, the New York Times reported to its hungry readers, "television set owners as far away as 50 miles viewed the action and heard the roar of the crowd."

Ex-player and Hall of Fame manager, Leo Durocher, was the starting shortstop for the Brooklyn Dodgers on that historic day and reflected kindly on his recollections of his managerial days in Ebbets Field. "It was Brooklyn against the world. They were not only complete fanatics, but they knew baseball like the fans of no other city. It was exciting to play there. It was a treat. I walked into that crummy, flyblown park as Brooklyn manager for nine years, and every time I entered, my pulse quickened and my spirits soared."

Fans and historians alike recall this next ground-breaking event as baseball's most memorable, as it changed not only the face of the game, but forced America to look inside itself and the direction the country was headed. President and General Manager Branch Rickey had previously signed, and eventually fielded, a player by the name of Jackie Robinson, and at 2:00 P.M., on April 15, 1947, Major League Baseball's first black player in the 20th Century hustled out to his position at first base. In Rickey's own words, "Ethnic prejudice has no place in sports, and baseball must recognize that truth if it is to maintain stature as a national game."

Perhaps no other ballpark, or the fans who unfailingly idolized their team, or the players who played the game, shared a romance of the heart as did Brooklyn, the Dodgers and Ebbets Field. Yankees fans, along with Fenway and Wrigley devotees, could conceivably argue this fact, but at this point in history, none of these three franchises have had their team and their hearts ripped out simultaneously.

After a 44-year love affair with the New York borough, a tragic act of thievery stole the team away to its new home in Los Angeles. For those who remember, the loss was devastating, with the effects still lingering to this day. As future Hall of Famer Pee Wee Reese once stated, "Brooklyn was the most wonderful city a man could play in, and the fans there were the most loyal there were." It's still considered by many to be nothing short of an unrivaled travesty in the annals of baseball history to have such an unwarranted act of treason bestowed upon the Brooklyn faithful. An act that would have their beloved Dodgers torn out from under them. Fans still believe their team was stolen from them and many fan clubs still exist carrying the hopes of one day having their franchise rightfully returned to them. The move was not approved because of a lack of attendance, as more than one million fans ushered themselves through the turnstiles in 1957, the last year Ebbets fielded a team. There was no argument as to the validity of placing teams on the West Coast, but simply put, many believe that existing commissioner, Ford C. Frick could have and should have intervened, awarding a team to Los Angeles while still maintaining the glorious franchise that was once the Brooklyn Dodgers.

The Dodgers played their last game at Ebbets Field on September 24, 1957, a 2-0 win over the visiting Pittsburgh Pirates. With their future already realized, only 6,702 fans attended this last historic event. Perhaps in a futile show of defiance, spectators stayed away in droves, their absence somehow, speaking louder than their presence.

When Ebbets field was torn down three years later in February, 1960, a large number of Dodger faithful including many ex-players, attended the final ceremonies precluding the demolition. As she had before many of the Brooklyn Dodger home games over the years, Lucy Monroe sang the National Anthem one last time.

~

SANCTUARY

Ebbets Field was a glorious sight
From Red Hook to Flatbush in style
A wall that carried to deep left field
Found the cobblestone tiles in right.

Italian marble enhanced the halls
With stitching that echoed throughout
Legends were framed in grass and dirt
In a sanctuary built for all.

Hearts will ignite and tend to accept
The flame of an eternal bond
In '58 that Dodger spark
Left Ebbets and Duke Snider wept.

An empty park now fills the days
The tears fall like bitter rain
History permeates and lingers
Like an eerie cool summer haze.

Gone, like a thief in the night
Brooklyn lies suspended in state
A fire yet burns and awaits the return
Ebbets Field was a glorious sight.

~ RWM

CHAPTER 10

~

BROOKS

A few years ago, I attended a sports card and collectors show in downtown Vancouver. I was never all that big into the collectibles scene as I was never all that big into spending money on cards I couldn't eat. Priorities. Cards and merchandise seemed a little pricey to me and besides, the market was saturated by then. Items worth acquiring were always out of my comfort zone, monetarily speaking. Autographs are great for the person who acquired them in the first place but it's not quite the same the second time around. When you think about it, was it actually that player's autograph on the card? Do we really know for sure? If the cards were, by chance, authenticated, well what do you know? They were even pricier. Even then, there was no guarantee that the name on the card was signed by that person.

A few months ago, I watched an undercover program where forgeries were taken to supposed experts for authentication. Quite a few were signed off as real autographs, which of course they weren't. It now seems to be nothing more than an educated guessing game. Of course players and celebrities alike change their signatures over time, whether knowingly or not, just as their personalities change with them. Age plays a small part as well, so who really knows except the person standing there getting it signed. All this makes a tough job even tougher to accomplish. Forgeries are rampant as the forgers are out to make a buck as well as the working stiffs who are out to make an honest living. Everybody has to eat.

Many of the vendors seemed a little full of themselves and held that air of self-importance. It was their day I guess, but I just didn't feel like I quite fit into that corner of the scene. The whole event was money driven, which to me, as the consumer, should not be the point. I know what you are thinking. "Show me the money" or "how do I make money" are two popular phrases, but the theme should always mirror the promotion of baseball or whatever the sport might be. Or more importantly, perhaps an investment in the future of the sport. An investment in the game we love and want to continue to see flourish.

We could all be spreading the proverbial word and doing our part to keep interest alive and the items circulating. After all, the sport is growing worldwide. With circulation and interaction the memorabilia game would garner more fan involvement for the present and down the road without the skyrocketing prices. Unfortunately profits are the name of the game. Get what you can now and forfeit the future. Go ahead! Water down the industry.

I admit I loved looking around at the older cards as it brought back a lot of memories. I could almost smell the bubble gum wrapped up in the old packs of brand new cards. There were plenty to buy but the gum had gone stale years before, if it was ever fresh to begin with. It was always hard to tell as the gum had the consistency of a thin sheet of glass. Overall, it was an enjoyable day spent with fond memories. A simpler time I guess. I've since rid myself of most of my own collection as I became tired of moving these items around every time I changed my address. I enjoyed this hobby in my own quiet way for a few years but have since moved on. Not grown up, just moved on.

I still have a small collection of old Baltimore Orioles favorites, including a couple of Topps, Cal Ripken, Jr. Rookie cards. A few Boog Powell and Eddie Murray cards as well but they are worth nothing close to the small fortune I had envisioned retiring on when I first started out. I first started watching baseball on television sometime after my days in Little League were over. Before that I was always told to go outside and find something to do. I would rather have parked my butt on the couch, put my favorite ball cap on and watched my heroes play. My parents always told me that if I wore my hat indoors all the time I would go bald. I now wish I had of worn it. I would then have an excuse. It's been some years since the girls have run their fingers through my hair. Let's just say my hair began to grow in a southerly direction. I'm proud that I have a face full of beard but upstairs nothing but a mosquito airport. I sometimes think back on the numerous TV and World Series games I missed. The history that surrounds them is something I will never get back. I guess you can't lose something you never had but at least I can read about it. Don't get me wrong, my lungs and I are forever thankful for all that historic fresh air. Speaking of Eddie Murray, as I look back, I can think of only two ballplayers that would have scared the crap out of me had I been a Major League pitcher. Chris Chambliss and Eddie Murray. The others I could have tolerated while they crushed whatever I threw to them but these two men were not only heavy-hitters and long ball threats every time they stepped into the batters box, they brought intimidation times ten to the plate. I can still picture Chambliss pointing his bat out at the pitcher as he stood in the batter's box. A warning of what was to come. I love these two guys and I just thought I would throw that out for some of you to chew on.

We've come a long way since sticking our favorite baseball player's trading card in our bicycle spokes because Bobby Richardson sounded cool at 20 mph. Now it just sounds annoying. But really, how many kids ride bikes nowadays anyway. The parents maybe, but let's face it, the kids get rides everywhere they go. Yeah I get the safety thing but literally, take a hike. Breathe in that historic fresh air. As for me, as far as baseball cards go, it's more about hanging on to personal favorites than bankrolling for the future.

I have to admit I really went to town on Frank Thomas at the start of his career and it paid off in a very small way with his recent induction into the Hall of Fame. Unfortunately, unless you've invested wisely and have some prized, high profile collectibles, and that right person who will lay down the dollars for them, you will never find wealth in selling them off. The market is saturated. If you do happen to own some of these rare, sought after collectibles? Congratulations! Once again, the rich get richer.

Thankfully the true fans, the ones with no money, are left with the true riches. The riches of youth, fond memories and a passion for the history of the game we sometimes find steeped in our own, very personal possessions. However small and inexpensive they may be. After all, when it comes right down to it, it's the thoughts that count. It's the thoughts and memories we've accumulated that survive and sustain us. I have to admit though, I am still lugging a few boxes of borderline memories around. I haven't quite got to that point where I can completely rid myself of these items without a tiny touch of seller's remorse although my lumbar sacral area is all for it.

Anyway, speaking of card shows, this particular show was being attended by none other than Brooks Robinson himself. Along with a few hockey names which of course I fail to remember. I have always loved Brooks and all the Orioles if the truth be known, so I decided to go down and see him in person. I couldn't believe the crowd this event drew, but then again, hockey was the lure in Canada. It always has been up in the frigid frozen. I quickly surmised where Mr. Robinson was seated and found out that I wasn't the only one who wanted to see the 1970 World Series MVP. He had somehow accumulated additional admirers. No kidding! He had won that award with a .429 batting average and broke the record at that time for hits in a World Series with seventeen. With that MVP award he was also awarded a brand new Toyota. Johnny Bench, from the losing Cincinnati Reds said after the Series, "If we had known he wanted a car that badly, we'd all have chipped in and bought him one."

When the lineup for autographs had finally cleared, I found myself face-to-face with not only a Hall of Famer, but one of the best defensive third basemen to ever play the game. A Baltimore Oriole no less. Yikes! Brooks Robinson! Throughout his entire career, he had always worn my own favorite number 5. I didn't mind as I'm pretty sure he had worn it first. After some nervous small talk, I waited patiently as he signed a couple of autographs for me, after which he stood to have his picture taken with me as well. What a thrill that must have been for him! He could hardly contain himself.

He was very engaging, laughed easy and was a real gentleman. Isn't it great when your heroes are still your heroes even after you meet them in person? Just before the picture was snapped, I asked him what it was like to play baseball for his manager, Earl Weaver. He just laughed and told me, "With Earl, you just score a lot of runs early and try to hang on." They both reside in the Baseball Hall of Fame. Apparently they both hung on.

Many people have commented on this great man's presence with very flattering remarks about his openness and accessibility. I now knew what they were talking about. I was so happy I had made the trip downtown. I still have the framed picture of the two of us and continue to carry his autograph with me regardless of where my next residence might be. He will forever remain one of the greatest performers to ever step on the field and for a few seconds I was a small part of his world. Just ask him, maybe he'll remember. I know I will.

Brooks and me sharing a laugh at a Vancouver card show.

~

Speaking of prized possessions, when I was around 12 years old, one of my bright summer days had suddenly got brighter when I came across a strange but welcome new addition to my small but budding baseball collection. My dad had taken on the coaching duties of my Little League team which is without question, extremely exciting for the coach's son. Yes, that was your cue to read between the lines. Along with the obvious duffel bags containing bats, catching equipment and lingering odors, we always had brand new baseballs, still wrapped and boxed, lying forever around the house. I have always loved the smell and feel of a brand new baseball and began to unwrap the box I had found on top of the refrigerator. To my absolute amazement, this lucky gem produced a baseball, autographed in fresh blue ink by none other than Mickey Mantle himself. What? I couldn't believe it! Was this the surprise lottery that Spalding had sponsored to see what lucky kid would unearth his hero's autograph? Did my dad buy this amazing gift for his number one son and best player on the team? Was I really that highly thought of? I was getting tingles all over. I could almost feel Mickey's presence right there in the kitchen beside me. I was getting a little carried away with my thoughts when I suddenly realized it was not Mickey's presence I had felt in the room. I turned to notice my older brother standing behind me and barely able to contain himself. His moment had arrived. Mine would have to wait. My vision of the Mick quietly dissipated, along with my fleeting sense of self-esteem. I had finally recognized my brother's handwriting. Very funny! At least he thought so.

What I thought was Mickey's autograph. I kept it anyway.

~

It's funny the things you remember about your playing days, but not so funny considering all that I've forgotten over the years. I played the game for 24 years at various levels so understandably there are some lost snippets still floating around in the dark somewhere up there. I'd like to think that little by little they will eventually come back to me. I can dream can't I? Every once in a while something jogs my memory and a little more sunlight comes trickling through. Things I haven't thought of in years.

In my last year of Little League, my team, the Athletics, had a pretty sharp 10-year-old playing second base for us. He was extremely enthusiastic and always seemed to have a smile on his face. It was entirely infectious and all the guys on the team really liked this new kid. He was ten but he looked like he was on loan from the Yankees.

During a League game one summer evening, on a routine ground ball hit past our first baseman and into shallow right field, the batter surprisingly rounded first base and took off for second. You just can't predict what kids will do. For 10 to 12 year olds, there was no logic or explanation required. There was no need or expectations for a cutoff, so of course our boy at second base saw what the runner was up to. He headed back to his bag and turned to look for the throw. I was playing short that day and was already at second but backed off to cover the play as our boy returned to his position. On the ensuing throw from our right fielder, there was an unexpected collision at second base and our 10-year-old phenom was literally knocked out cold. I noticed the ball still in his glove and introduced it as exhibit number one to the base ump. I called time as our players and coaches gathered around. After a brief period, he finally blinked a few times and came to. He opened his eyes and the first thing he said was, "Is he out?" I couldn't believe it! I looked around for the movie cameras. Keep them rolling. Flat on his back and the outcome of the play was the first thing that came to mind. That's all he wanted to know.

It was all about the game for him, even at that age. After the tag, our boy had held onto the ball even as he fell. The runner in fact, was definitely out. In fact, they had both been out, but in completely different ways. As the years trickle by, for some reason, that play always sticks out in my mind. It was plain and simple. A flat out love for the game. He had it locked up inside him. I had always envisioned that particular scenario was something you would see in a movie or read about in a book, but it happened. I was there.

~

I was always on the short side of tall and remain so to this day. Shortstop had seemed like the obvious position for me and as it turned out, I was pretty good at it. I enjoyed infield practice almost as much as I enjoyed the games. Almost! I was also starting to listen to a lot of music in the mid-sixties. A great time for expanding horizons, developing tastes and playing pool. My dad had bought a homemade 6x12 slate pool table and it was a beauty. The guy that sold it had built it in his basement and apparently never thought about getting rid of it. He had to rip off the frame and door jams just to get it out to our truck. He must have really needed the money, although I'm sure a fair chunk of it was spent on repairs. I doubt if he broke even but I hope he appreciated the extra room he had.

The table had a rough finish but great rubber and gorgeous felt covering. It was a beautifully built homemade table and it fit nicely in our basement. We had enough room for almost all of our shots. Navigating a wall was a small challenge but a much shorter cue took care of the rest. I was a pretty fair player as I got a lot of practice, but my brother was a natural. We got together at a local pool hall a few years back and played ten games of 8-ball. He won nine. He sewered on the eight ball but I give myself full marks for my one win. I didn't think I would ever beat him and I won't let him forget it.

We had a transistor radio downstairs and it was always tuned into C-FUN, which at that time was one of Vancouver's great music stations. I loved all the new music I was hearing and couldn't get enough of the Beatles, The Who, The Beach Boys, Paul Revere and the Raiders, The Four Tops and everything the British Invasion could send over. It seemed like everyone you knew either played the guitar or was taking lessons. My next door neighbor was a great guitar player and eventually sent himself to the Berklee School of music in Boston a few years later. It was the drums for me. I just loved the idea of beating on those skins the way Ringo, Keith Moon, and Ginger Baker did, although they eventually made more money at it than I did.

I had just turned 13 years old and I discovered that I had been the first player taken in the draft which graduated all the older Little Leaguers into Babe Ruth. I was the All-Star shortstop and not a bad pitcher but first overall didn't really mean that much to me at that point. It did seem pretty important to my dad though. This was the big time now. Bigger fields, bigger kids, leadoffs, longer base paths, and a new mound which was now the regulation 60 feet 6 inches. It seemed about three feet higher and a hundred feet further from the plate than I was used to. And the stretch. Aahh, the stretch. Nobody had ever told me when I was on the mound about going into the stretch with a runner on base. I'm pretty sure that is what practices are for. A little instruction please! Maybe they thought I was such a great pitcher that nobody would ever get on base for my three years in the League. They were wrong! It turned out the new coaches just thought I knew what I was doing. I didn't! Time was called and a crash course on how to pitch with runners on was conducted right there on the mound. A little embarrassing for the supposed whiz kid. Where was the instruction or the communication. Hello?

As it turned out, the outfield fences were so far from home plate, you'd have to pack a lunch if the ball was hit out there. With all that came the new pressures I was starting to put on myself. I wasn't feeling up to it to tell you the truth. I really loved baseball but I was finding new friends and lots of different things to do with my time. Again, read between the lines.

What it came down to was, I really wanted a new set of drums and one day I figured I might as well just come right out and ask for a set. My sister was taking piano lessons and we had a beautiful big piano sitting right downstairs for whenever she wanted to play. Which I knew for a fact was hardly ever. She really didn't want to take lessons. She wanted to play the piano but just didn't want to go through the learning process. That seemed entirely logical to me. But here I was, actually willing to learn to play an instrument, so in all fairness; shouldn't I be rewarded as well? Pretty sound thinking on my end, but it wasn't that easy.

My dad reminded me that baseball was going to be taking up a lot of my time and taking drum lessons and practicing as much as I would have to just wasn't going to be possible at that particular moment in time. It was becoming clear that my decisions were being made for me. Didn't he know that I was a teenager now and could make my own decisions? I found out the answer to that question pretty quick as well. I mean, what he said had made perfect sense. Deep down I knew I would be playing baseball. There was no logical reason why I wouldn't be. Isn't it funny how you end up liking things that you turn out to be good at? What a strange coincidence!

Everybody wants to be good at something and everybody is good at something. You just have to find it. It's tough to stay away from something that you do which really impresses people. Maybe it's ego and maybe it's just wanting to please others, but oddly enough, for the most part, you tend to stay close to anything you have a talent for.

As far as playing the drums and getting my parents to actually spring for a set, I hadn't really got to that point where I was cunning enough to play one side of the coin against the other. Baseball for drums. I have to admit, it would have been a much better story if I told you that it was all planned. But it wasn't.

After work one day, my dad came up to me and said he had a deal he would like to make that I might be interested in. I was still oblivious to the obvious. My mom and dad would buy me a set of drums if I agreed to play baseball this coming Spring. I have to believe that deep down, they knew I was going to play regardless. One way or the other I was going to be in uniform come opening day. I guess they just wanted it to be my decision. Or at least make it seem that way. At thirteen I had no union to back me up so if they had given me the word that I was playing baseball and that was that, then, yes, that would have been that. But they didn't play it that way and years later I came to appreciate the way they had handled it.

As it turned out, I came away with a great sense of rhythm and a love for music that I am thankful for and still have to this day. I ended up playing baseball for another twenty years and after a year or so, the drums were looking like a natural fit sitting in the corner of the basement. My own musical shrine. A shout out to the Sixties. As far as the music it goes without saying, we were a far cry from the Jackson family.

I tend to look back on baseball and the good times I had playing the game more than I do the times spent jamming with Led Zeppelin or Steely Dan. Which was never. I really liked the drums and wished I had pursued it more vigorously. But at that particular time in this boy's life, there was a choice to be made. One or the other. I'm thankful for the direction I took, and am also thankful in no small part to my parents who, whether knowingly or not, steered me in the right direction. As far as longevity goes, I am aware of more early deaths in rock stars than baseball stars. I have to admit though, that with the recent use of steroids in today's game, somewhere

down the road, if it is not cleaned up, I am afraid that the statistics will
begin to even out.

~

Coquitlam Little League 1964, 11 years old (me holding the bat, #5)
(Photo by The Stride Studios)

~

CHAPTER 11

~

THE GREATEST

As history will confirm, a great many players have suited up to play Major League Baseball. As a matter of fact, approximately 18,000 players have taken part in America's national pastime throughout the years. Although many of them have obviously come and gone, the ultimate decision and the age-old argument of perhaps, who was the greatest all-round player, has come no closer to its conclusion than the first time the question arose. It's an impossible road to travel as we attempt to determine who might once and for all, be the greatest baseball player in the history of the game.

As you can well imagine, various names and ensuing careers, past and present, have been thrown into the ring for the fans and pundits to ponder. One glaring point that stands out for me is that a great many of these players bear an uncanny resemblance to each other in the fact that most of them played the outfield for the better part of their careers. The three prominent names on almost everybody's list include Joe DiMaggio, Willie Mays and Mickey Mantle. I'm sure I've raised some eyebrows already but that only serves to underline the debate. The one obvious reason for the prominence of outfielders in the selection process is that they outnumber every other position by a 3-1 count. It hardly seems fair but that fact alone helps to clarify the road we are travelling down. But is that one fact enough to quench our curiosities and suffice the intellectual needs required in order for us to answer this very important question? There have been literally thousands of other unquestionable greats, and oddly enough, they plied their wares at positions other than the land beyond the infield.

With the amazing number of talented superstars that have played the game and continue to play to this day, the argument still hangs over us like a black cloud. This outfield majority seems to me a little more than just mere coincidence. I suppose, to further bolster the outfield standpoint, we could certainly add the names of Roberto Clemente, Ted Williams, Stan Musial, Al Kaline, the incomparable Babe Ruth and of course, the great Ty Cobb. For the young guns of today's game and tomorrow's history, dare I mention Yasiel Puig or Mike Trout? Jose Fernandez or Giancarlo Stanton of the Miami Marlins? The list goes on. My regrets to those I've offended by not listing their names. Certainly, there are baseball legends that I may have inadvertently omitted for the sake of ink, but those players have not, and will never be forgotten. Hopefully the names I've included here are enough to make the point. The very same mistake of omission will be made as I address the position players.

Speaking of which, we now ask ourselves, why hasn't a first baseman, a third baseman, shortstop or catcher been on this short list of the greatest players ever? The names are obvious standouts as well, but their absence in the final countdown are surely innocent as we continue to speculate. As we break down the numbers however, they become less puzzling. Don't get me wrong, all are worthy candidates and deserve to be included in this process. The strong throws from right or center field are no less intimidating than a strong throw from third base, deep in the hole at shortstop, or a quick release from behind the plate. What about the player with the high on-base percentage or the consummate base stealer? And what about the player that accrues an incredible amount of extra base hits throughout his career or even predominantly singles hitters such as Rod Carew or Tony Gwynn? Surely, this is a valuable commodity for any winning formula.

I am a long way from dismissing the idea of the title going to an outfielder, but hey, being able to run all out in the spacious grass domain provided for them to track down a fly ball, or dive to make an impossible catch, or crash into an outfield wall for the almighty out, are neither unique nor exclusive to that position. Brooks Robinson, to throw one name down, has arguably made more exciting plays on line drives or groundballs than anyone else in the game. Playoffs included! And yes, that is important. When the chips are down, some rise to the top while others simply fade from view. Who could disagree about the value of dazzling shortstops like Ozzie Smith, Derek Jeter or the steady play of Honus Wagner or the Iron Man, Cal Ripken? Joe Morgan and Ryne Sandberg are just two of the names that come to mind for second base. What about the all-round play of third baseman Mike Schmidt, who went from having the lowest batting average of any regular starting player one year, to arguably the best third baseman to ever play the game. Hold on! I'm sure there are hairs bristling on the back of many George Brett fans, (myself included) with that statement. And rightly so! Brett was not only one of the most well-respected players to ever suit up for the game, but one of its very best. He was extremely productive and even more so when the game was on the line. Clutch-hitting is a valuable asset and shouldn't be taken lightly when narrowing down the elite. Fan favorites, believe it or not, also play a role in the ultimate process. With so many players vying for the title of "the greatest ever," let's face it, popularity plays a huge role.

Speaking of popular, another well-respected player that will forever grace our memories and the games' history was Lou Gehrig. No surprise there, and it wasn't just his "...luckiest man on the face of the earth," speech. His statistics and outstanding play speak volumes about the man. Who knows what he might have accomplished or even greater esteem he might be held in had he not been taken from us well before his time. Once again, speaking of popularity, the name Ted Williams presents itself. Unlike George Brett and Lou Gehrig, he wasn't exactly the most popular man with the media, or, should the truth be known, even the hometown fans in Boston. He was to many, however, THE greatest hitter to ever wear a uniform. All you had to do was ask Ted himself for the answer to that question.

Perhaps a man for all seasons, and positions, was one of the greatest players ever. We should be considering him as well when throwing together a list of the game's elite. Pete Rose played almost everywhere on the field and was the epitome of pure unadulterated hustle. His desire for winning was unmatched. You can bet on it! Conversely, in my humble opinion, considering other nominees we've seen enshrined, I'm sure Pete's lack of popularity is perhaps one of the reasons he is not in the Hall of Fame today.

What a shame! Off the field, I could take him or leave him but as a ballplayer, few deserve induction more than he. I will now take this opportunity to salute him! (And while I'm at it, I might as well cast my vote for Shoeless Joe as well.) So, what attribute should move to the forefront as we consider our most valuable of determining factors in the race for the almighty title? Sure we all love the home run, and of course our team must score to win. After all, isn't winning what it's all about? Well, not so much, if in fact, we are attempting to place one player's status above all others. Hall of Famer Andre Dawson won the 1987 MVP award while playing for the last place Chicago Cubs.

Championships mean a lot but don't forget, while one team is busy manufacturing runs, the other team is trying to stop them. At the same time, they are trying to squeeze at least one more run out of their own lineup to try and win the game. Let's not forget, the losing teams in the championship games have some pretty great players as well. So shouldn't it make sense that stopping the aforementioned team from initiating any kind of scoring spree be just as important? Shouldn't defense be just as important as offense? And keeping with that theory, shouldn't a topnotch, big-game, low ERA, strikeout pitcher be high on our most valuable list? Ah, but as you rightly point out, we are talking about all-round players! Are we not? Starting pitchers pitch every four or five days and only bat in the National League or Interleague play, so there are roughly 130 games in which their participation is absolutely zero. Sure they cheer from the top step, occasionally pinch run and more times than not, stop losing streaks. Sure a lot of them tutor the younger players, but many of them rarely see the batter's box feet first. Besides, they have their own category should that question arise. Best Pitcher of all time! Okay, I know; reliever, closer, set up guy, starter? That's a whole other chapter. Mariano Rivera is admittedly the best closer ever, hands down, but the best player ever? So, what about the guys that score the runs? Rickey Henderson and Ty Cobb are perhaps among the greatest ever to top that list. Their job was to get on base. Do we care how they do it? No, we do not!

So, what ever happened to defense? It has been said that a pitcher's best friend is the double play and that's true. It is! They are game changers! Three run homers don't hurt either, but every team needs strength up the middle. And what about the corner infielders who dive to stop the extra-base hits, or the blocked pitch by the underrated and overworked catchers who save the runs or stop runners from moving into scoring position. Defense is an integral part of the winning tradition most organizations expect but don't always get. Shouldn't these players who perform miracles with their gloves deserve some recognition as well? Defense, unfortunately, seems to be a lost art as far as fan appreciation or contractual obligation goes. I'm not saying it is overlooked, as most true fans and a lot of the players embrace all aspects of the game. We just don't get as much to pick from anymore. Perhaps defense is taken for granted but not fully consummated, and in my opinion, routine plays should be. These are Major Leaguers. These players are supposed to be the elite of the elite. Truly talented sports figures are supposed to be looked up to for what they accomplish on the field and off! Someone we would like to emulate and admire. They need to be more complete players to earn that respect.

Most ballplayers, unless you are a left-handed pitcher or a switch-hitting catcher, understand that a good bat is most likely their ticket to the Major Leagues. Owners, General Managers, managers and scouts must all share the burden of guilt as far as rewarding offense over defense, instead of the combination of the two. Saving a run in my eyes is, for lack of a better term, a defensive RBI. Sadly, defensive mediocrity has been deemed acceptable far too often. Perhaps it's time for a new statistic. Maybe we should look to the NHL and keep track of a player's plus/minus for run production and runs allowed. One error can lead to multiple runs against, change a pitcher's outing and the game itself completely. Time to keep track of who is responsible and how often.

It's not off the wall to think that learning to hit is much more difficult to master than the skills needed for defensive excellence. As the experts say, trying to hit a round ball with a round bat and hit it square is one of the most difficult achievements to aspire to in any sport. Maybe the baseball brain trust has decided that if hitting skills or the potential for it exists in a player, then defense can be gained through simple instruction. Sounds great in theory but it's usually too late for excellence so we settle for good enough. Which it isn't. I've lost count of the times infielders (particularly third basemen) refuse to get in front of the ball particularly with runners in scoring position. Far too many times they stand aside and wave at it as it goes by. Block it and save the run! Just like we were all taught! And I'm tired of the analysts coming up with half-baked reasons for their lack of defensive abilities. Scorekeepers also need to turn their own performance up a notch. I can't believe the number of base hits that are given that should be errors. These are grown men. They are well aware of the errors they make and I'm sure they can live with it. It might even motivate them to take some extra ground balls.

While I'm on the subject, and believe me this is not meant to discredit Derek Jeter because, well, how can you? He just happened to be the central figure in a play that epitomizes exactly what I am talking about. It also helps me to air the point I would like to make. On August 18, 2014, in the first inning of a game against the Cleveland Indians, Jeter tied Honus Wagner for sixth on the all-time hit list. Good for him. There was just no way this was not going to happen. If not this night, then the next. It's how it happened that burns me up. Don't get me wrong, it was not his fault. He swings the bat, hits the ball and it plays itself out. It was a ground ball up the middle that shortstop Jose Ramirez handled cleanly on the grass, spun and threw to first base. It was not an easy play but one a pro ballplayer is expected to make. As first baseman Carlos Santana (no, not that one) stretched out for the catch, the ball leveled in just slightly above his head. Obviously a catchable ball. His foot was on the bag and as the announcer remarked, he just dropped it. If he catches it as he should have, Jeter is out easily by a step. At the time it was declared a base hit and I just about choked. You could tell by the pitchers reaction that the play should have been made. It was an error. No problem, it happens every day. I'm sure Santana knew it as well. A few days later the call was reversed and Jeter's 3,000th was given for a hit he got the following day. Because of the high profile I'm sure Major League Baseball stepped in to make the correct call. At the time, I thought I'd have to look elsewhere to make my point but it was such an opportune moment that even after the fact, I will continue.

Now here's where Derek Jeter could have immortalized himself to every baseball fan in the country. I would have loved to see him call time and with a smile, casually walk towards the home plate umpire, point to the press box where the official score keeper sits, wave off the hit and quietly state his case to the man in blue. Not on a personal level but a baseball level. Take a page out of Paul Waner's book and ask to have the play scored as an error as it should have been called in the first place. It wouldn't have mattered if they didn't change the call, his point would have been made. The gesture would have been talked about for years to come. In 1942, Waner disputed a call when the scorekeeper gave him a hit which at the time would have been his 3,000th. He stated later that he wanted it to be a clean hit, not tainted, which clearly showed his pride and integrity. If Waner had the national coverage and social media outlets we have today, he would have been a star by anyone's standards. Perhaps everyone would know who he was and what he did.

You can make the case that maybe Jeter didn't want to show up another player for making an error, but again, these are grown men. They'll get over it. Derek prides himself on keeping a low profile and for not saying the wrong thing or creating any kind of controversy. Great idea and it works for him, especially playing in New York. But coming clean would have sealed his legacy even more. It would not only have been a noble gesture but the right thing to do for him and baseball. The baseball world as a whole would have collectively dropped their jaws in awe. It would have been headlines for weeks. Not only that, but it would then shed some light on the often shoddy score keeping that we are accustomed to. Perhaps then the League could move ahead a little bit more in its approach to solidify its integrity. It would have at least started the dialogue. I know hits and errors are sometimes overturned but not nearly enough to justify the play or the stats. After all, the League is very interested in statistics. It helps to keep a high profile and showcase the tremendously talented players in Major League Baseball. They are all of that and deserve praise for their accomplishments. But they don't need it to be tainted. Do it right! Whew!! That's a load off my mind. For better or for worse, the introduction of replay cameras will render this discussion and others like it obsolete. Thank you for bearing with me. In closing, I really hope someday someone takes a stand and emulates Hall of Famer Paul Waner. Baseball deserves it!

I believe that defense should be hammered into players as youngsters and should be mastered by the time they reach the Big Leagues. You shouldn't arrive without the skills or lose it once you get there. And why can't anybody bunt nowadays? Again, fundamentals. I understand the pressures of the moment, but please! You are supposed to be the best of the best. A bunt can contribute to a team win just as much as a home run. I'm tired of the announcers building these guys up, almost idol chasing, but when a mistake is made, give excuses for their soft play. They screwed up! It happens! Just say so! Maybe it's true that some announcers feel they won't be granted interviews with certain players they have criticized the night before. Well, if the players won't talk to you, report that on the evening sports and tell the audience why! It's time to start telling it like it is.

For some final thoughts, since we were small kids, grabbing a bat and staring down the pitcher is what we all dreamed about. Everybody wants their chance at the plate and rightly so. Does that make offense and the art of hitting a baseball more important? Well, yes and no! Ultimately, the only answer to our question is to gather all the information we can, put it all together and try and squeeze out your ultimate candidate for top honors. But that creates our next problem. The real question then becomes, who is right and who is wrong? The short answer is, well, no one! On the other hand, everyone is! Simply stated, it should all come back to the one remaining principle, which states that the greatest ever, should have a repertoire comprised of all the tools and know how to use them. Perhaps then and only then will we have the best all-round baseball player we so desperately seek. So, where does that leave us? Unfortunately, right back where we started!

I do apologize if I've led you down the garden path. I have no more redeeming intangibles for observation, qualifications or conclusions than anyone else that might attempt to enlighten fans on the subject. You have your own insights and I have mine. If any of us truly care, and I think we do, we have already nurtured profound opinions of our own. If you don't care then you've probably stopped reading a long time ago. Those of us, who are the least bit concerned regarding the answer to these questions about baseball supremacy, have already drawn our own conclusions. And with the access to information nowadays, I must say, we have reached these conclusions with increasingly informed points of view. I've raised these questions for that very reason. Help me find the answer. All the questions and all the answers lay within each and every one of us, as we all have our favorite players and our own idea of who should be the final piece of this puzzle. Whether past or present, each of our worthy candidates performed with their own various skills, or in many cases, all of the aforementioned skills and then some. As Leo Durocher once claimed, the perfect ballplayer must possess five major attributes. They include the ability to run, throw, catch, hit, and hit with power and any other intangibles they might bring to the ballpark. Sounds easy enough, doesn't it?

While the answer you arrive at might be acceptable for your own passions and intellect, getting the baseball world as a whole to agree with you is next to impossible. That is the nature of the beast and just one of the many reasons why the game of baseball remains to me and to many like me, undoubtedly, the greatest sport on earth. The discussions we have will be ongoing for years and years, or at least I hope so! The one fact that we can all agree on is that we will always disagree. And that, my friend, is the core of it in a nutshell. Statistics! Where would we be without them? They fuel the fire. This topic, this quest for the best and countless others have been discussed, argued and debated without a definitive answer for decades. I'm positive it will continue for many more. Therein lies the absolute beauty of the game. How can you not be romantic about baseball?

~

THE SHOES

Joe DiMaggio...
Just look at his shoes,
He toyed with fly balls
He couldn't spell lose.

Yankee pinstripes,
Where few men belong
A true man of legend,
Immortalized in song.

A brilliant career
He knew it was done
But few will compare
To history's own son.

His peers sit in awe
Man, what a hitter!
Only one Joltin' Joe,
Only one Yankee Clipper!

~ RWM

CHAPTER 12

~

THE REAL THING

Joseph Paul DiMaggio was born November 25, 1914 in Martinez, California, a small town approximately 20 miles north of Oakland. Eighteen years later while playing for a Minor League team in San Francisco, he gave us a hint of what was in store for not only himself but baseball fans the world over. In 1933, a few short months before his nineteenth birthday, Joe had at least one hit in an unbelievable 61 consecutive games. How could anyone have possibly conceived that in eight years' time, while playing for the New York Yankees, he would set a Major League record that still stands to this day. A record that most observers believe will not be broken in this lifetime. A hitting streak that is as alive today as it was in 1941. His 56 straight games is a feat that even the brightest hitters in this or any era can't even begin to fathom. Most baseball experts agree, it is the one record that will never be broken. Lou Gehrig's consecutive games played streak of 2,131 was supposedly untouchable as well, I admit. Cal Ripken, Jr. demolished that record on September 6, 1995, so to quote a much used baseball phrase, you never know. Ripken's mark reached 2,632 before he sat himself out of his final home game of the season against the New York Yankees on September 20, 1998.

DiMaggio's streak began on May 15, 1941 against pitcher Cotton Ed Smith and the Chicago White Sox before coming to an abrupt halt on July 17. It would be a gross understatement to suggest numerous memorable events occurred on the days in between which helped to shape this momentous occasion. In spring training earlier that same year, in perhaps a forecast of things to come, Joe hit safely in every exhibition game. He kept up this torrid pace and carried it through to the first eight games of the season, until a junkball pitcher named Lester McCrabbe of the Philadelphia Athletics, literally threw him into a funk. Joe's average had fallen below the .300 mark by mid-May until that storied day, when a weak single off pitcher Cotton Ed Smith started him on the road to infamy. He never looked back.

It was not DiMaggio's string of consecutive games which fans first began to notice because, who knew? It was more the fact that his average was now climbing once again. He was garnering attention as a worthy opponent to Ted Williams and ultimately the bragging rights for the 1941 batting title. Williams would go on to win the title with a spectacular .406 average. The last year any champion, or any batter finished a season over .400. As well as the batting crown, Williams slugged 37 home runs producing 120 RBI, 135 runs scored, with an on base percentage of .551. A remarkable season! In contrast, DiMaggio finished the season with a .357 mark adding 125 RBI with 30 homers, and an on base percentage of .440. These statistics seem to fall somewhat short of Williams' efforts. Many thought he had a better overall year than Joe, but DiMaggio was voted the Most Valuable Player award in 1941.

Ted Williams had never bridged the distance between himself and the Boston faithful who, over the years, had taken a dislike to his surly demeanor. The fans booed him, and in return, he ignored not only them, but the sports writers who covered the Red Sox team as well. He refused to speak to the press and many believe this contributed to his own demise as far as certain awards were concerned. Considering a three-year absence during the peak of his career in which he served his country in World War II, Williams' career totals are nothing short of astonishing. He collected 2,654 hits, including 521 home runs, 1,839 RBI, and a .344 lifetime batting average in 2,292 games. Although he did win two Most Valuable Player awards in 1946 and 1949, his Triple Crown years of 1942 and 1947 failed to earn him the MVP award in either of those standout years. His six American League batting titles did not escape the attention of the Hall of Fame however, and his induction finally arrived in 1966, his first year of eligibility.

There is no disputing the numbers DiMaggio produced in 1941. (As well as winning the MVP in 1941, he put his name on two more. Those coming in 1939 and 1947.) The 56-game streak certainly enhanced his stature among the voters, but his first place finish that year was, to many fans, more than warranted and contributed immensely to his impressive Hall of Fame credentials. To the Yankee fans that saw him play, there was no one better.

Babe Ruth's last year as a Yankee came in 1934. Lou Gehrig's last year was 1939, but he was limited to only eight games that season before giving way to amyotrophic lateral sclerosis. The seemingly immortal Lou Gehrig gave his "...luckiest man in the world..." speech July 4, 1939 and died almost two years later on June 2, 1941. To this day, Gehrig is one of the most respected men in the history of the game.

The New York fans had been spoiled for many years by the performances of both Ruth and Gehrig, amongst many others, but they were now witnessing the amazing exploits of their latest Yankee phenom. The day Lou Gehrig passed away, Joe's consecutive game streak had reached nineteen, with two hits off of future Hall of Fame and Cleveland Indians pitcher, Bob Feller. People were starting to take notice and New York again was the place to be!

The record books were now being torn wide open as DiMaggio's streak ran through the twenties. The last time fans had visited such an event was in 1922, when George Sisler's 41 straight games, broke Ty Cobb's American League mark of 40, set in 1911. Wee Willie Keeler still held the National League record of 44 games which he had set many years earlier, back in 1897. (Sisler would eventually mount another assault on Keeler's record in 1925, but fell short at a still impressive 34 games.) In 1894, Bill Dahlen, while playing for the Chicago Colts, (as the Cubs were called then) gained notoriety with a 42-game hitting streak, but for some reason, was not recognized as a player to be reckoned with in the overall scheme of things.

The only possible guess for his omission at that time, was that reporters had assumed his streak had come at a time when the distance from the mound to home plate was different than its present day 60 feet 6 inches. They couldn't have been more wrong. In 1893, only one year before, the distance was changed from 55 feet 6 inches, to its present length, which meant that Dahlen's name should have been acknowledged at the very least. Although it was still short of Keeler's record, DiMaggio's next target should have been Dahlen's total, which fell between Sisler and Wee Willie's. This error has since been clarified and is now a part of the record books. He deserved a better fate and should have been remembered at that time.

There was some controversy as DiMaggio's streak edged closer to 30 games. In 1941, Dan Daniel, a renowned sports writer and editor, provided his services as the official score keeper for games at Yankee Stadium as well as covering the road games for his newspaper the World Telegram. He saw every game during the streak and was the official scorekeeper for more than twenty of them and wrote continually about it. Almost everyone wanted DiMaggio to break the record, and avid Yankee supporters demanded hits no matter how glaring the error might have been. The opposing players were also nervous when Joe came to the plate during this period, as no one wanted to be caught dogging it on a ball he had hit, therefore, extending the streak.

On June 17, while facing Johnny Rigney of the Chicago White Sox, Joe hit a grounder to shortstop, Luke Appling. While moving towards the ball, it suddenly took a bad hop and hit the infielder square in the shoulder. Now in a rush, Appling grabbed the ball, dropped it, and then finally threw to first a split second too late. Daniel ruled it a hit! It was Joe's only hit of the day! He came up again in the ninth inning and was robbed of a home run by outfielder Taft Wright, who literally snatched it out of the right field stands. DiMaggio would have gone hitless that day if not for the ruling. The streak had now reached 30 games. The following day, as Yogi Berra once said, was like déjà vu all over again. Appling again was on the receiving end of Joe's hard hit grounder which, this time he could only knock down. No throw was made. Too hot to handle was Daniel's ruling. The quest was still alive. Joe had no hand in the scorekeeper's decisions. He just went out every day and played the game like it was supposed to be played. One player summed up DiMaggio's ability in one easy sentence: "He never did anything wrong on the field." That statement would speak volumes for Joe's entire thirteen-year Major League career.

By the time Rogers Hornsby's 34-game streak had been surpassed, most of America was caught up in the excitement. Les Brown and his orchestra released a recording entitled "Joltin' Joe DiMaggio", a less than memorable song, but to no one's surprise, it was embraced by the Yankee throngs. None other than Bill "BoJangles" Robinson attended the games at Yankee Stadium and entertained the fans while dancing on the dugout roof in between innings. He even sprinkled what he called "goofer dust" around, hoping it would bring Joltin' Joe further luck. It seemed to work! The streak seemed to take the pressure off the rest of his teammates, and the Yankees continued to cruise into baseball's spotlight. Resuming their place in history, they would soon take the 1941 World Series in five games over their cross town rival, the Brooklyn Dodgers.

George Sisler's record fell at Washington's Griffith Stadium on June 29, in a double-header against the Senators. Joe tied his mark with one hit in the first game off Dutch Leonard, and one more off of Arnold Anderson in the night cap. They were the only two hits he had all day, and the only two hits he would need. Wee Willie Keeler and the top of the list were now a mere two games away.

The hit which tied Keeler's record was accompanied by a little bit of luck; it came during the second game of a double-header against the Boston Red Sox. Fortunately for Joe, the hit happened early in the game, as a down-pour later soaked Yankee Stadium. The game was called after five innings but official nonetheless. During the rain delay, a souvenir seeker apparently reached over the dugout fence and stole a bat, which turned out to be none other than DiMaggio's favorite stick. He was not a man to be easily upset and the next day, borrowed a bat from teammate Tommy Henrich. The bat was so chosen for its unique similarities, and its 36-inch, 36-ounce dimensions. Joe went one for five that day and finally broke the record with a long home run off nineteen-game winner Dick Newsome. A ball that ironically, soared high over the head of long-time rival Ted Williams. Joe DiMaggio now stood alone atop the heap.

For the past 56 days, the streak had caused considerable pressure on so many involved with its existence. None more than Joe himself. With the new record in his pocket, the pressure was at last lifted. As if he hadn't been already, DiMaggio began to hit like a man possessed. He collected 25 hits in his next twelve games before the streak's inevitability would finally catch up with him on July 17. He had passed the 50-game mark with ease, but once again Joe would meet Johnny Rigney, this time in the 54th game. Chicago third baseman Bob Kennedy was playing a typically deep hot corner, as many had done for the hard swinging DiMaggio. This proved to be fruitful for Joe on this day, but would ironically lead to his undoing in the 57th game! He swung hard and topped a roller down the line and beat it out for a single. Game 54 was in the books.

During a ride to the game on July 17, an interesting premonition occurred involving a Cleveland cab driver. Apparently, the cabbie half-turned to Joe in the backseat and said, "I've got a feeling that if you don't get a hit your first time up tonight, they're going to stop you." Teammate Lefty Gomez, sharing the cab with Joe that day, seemed more upset by the remark than DiMaggio. The startled Gomez replied, "Who the hell are you?" Taken aback, perhaps not knowing what else to say, Lefty continued, "What are you trying to do, jinx him?" Joe seemed unfazed by the incident.

Cleveland pitchers Al Smith and Jim Bagby, Jr. later reveled in the fact they had combined to shut down Joltin' Joe, but in fact, it was the glove and positioning of Ken Keltner at third base that had diffused this Bronx bomber. Joe drilled two shots down the line that Keltner turned into two outs. Third base was a wall that unfortunately had unforgiving tendencies on this day. The luck that had befriended DiMaggio during the streak, now turned against him in his last at bat. A ball seemingly headed up the middle, took a funny bounce, and somehow ended up in Lou Boudreau's glove. He quickly flipped to second baseman Ray Mack, starting a double play which shut down any chance of the streak continuing. It was over!

After the game, Joe and Keltner signed the sweet spot of the game ball with the third baseman further writing, "I got a police escort out of the stadium after stopping Joe's 56-game hitting streak." On the other side, Boudreau signed it and wrote, "Started the double play that ended Joe's 56-game streak." Joe was not one to hold a grudge or carry any bitterness over such things. All the soft spoken man had to say was, "I wish it could have gone on forever." Don't we all! In the years to come, countless more would attest to witnessing the end of the magic in Municipal Stadium that day, but in fact there were 67,648 divided fans that saw an amazing piece of history laid to rest.

The streak had been stopped but Joe DiMaggio had not. A guilt stricken fan from Newark had even returned Joe's stolen bat. He used it the next day and started another streak which ended at a modest sixteen games. Once again, Bill Dahlen's name quietly rose to the forefront. In 1894, after his string of 42 consecutive games in which he had a hit, Dahlen had rattled off another 28 games. The oft forgotten man had left in his wake an unbelievable streak of 70 out of 71 games in which he had collected at least one hit. The Yankee Clipper still had him beat! Joe had hit safely in 72 of 73 contests!

During DiMaggio's monument to consistency, his statistics were amazing. In those 56 games and 223 at bats, Joe had 91 hits, with 15 home runs (half his season's total), and 55 RBI. He batted .408, had 22 multi-hit games, including five three-hit games, and four four-hit games. He had 35 extra base hits, 56 runs scored, was hit by a pitch twice, and struck out only seven times. It's no wonder he won the MVP award over Williams, although it was a closely contested race. Towards the end of that year, on December 7, 1941, the Japanese bombed Pearl Harbor and America became involved in WWII. Before the 1942 season began, Joe was asked to take a $2,500 pay cut, and although he eventually managed a $5,000 increase, it was to be his last season until 1946. Joe entered military service, and served there for three years.

Joe DiMaggio retired after the 1951 season with outstanding credentials, and a record most baseball experts say will never be broken. Thirty years later, Joe spoke of the prophetic taxi driver in Cleveland during that 1941 season, who had somehow recently approached him, "The guy said he was that cab driver. He apologized and he was serious. I felt awful. He might have been spending his whole life thinking he had jinxed me, but I had told him he hadn't. My number was up!" A gentleman to the end!

Before his death on March 8, 1999, he was often referred to as "The greatest ballplayer alive." Many fans still consider him in that regard. Joe DiMaggio was elected to the Baseball Hall of Fame in Cooperstown, New York, in 1955, his first year of eligibility.

****

"The very mention of his name personifies class, dignity, elegance and professionalism both on and off the field. A true gentleman, he will always be the standard to which all great baseball players are measured."

—*Yankee broadcaster Tim McCarver*

"As a kid growing up in New York, I remember all the street corner arguments about Mantle and Mays, and invariably, somebody from my father's generation would chime in with 'Hey, Willie's great, and Mickey can hit a ball over a building, but you never saw DiMaggio, kid. You never saw the real thing.'"

—*Sportscaster Bob Costas*

~

As a tribute to Joe DiMaggio's tremendous 56-game hitting streak, the following is a 56-line poem dedicated to the man, and a record that will never be broken.

56!

The first hit came on May fifteenth,
A seeing-eye single at best.
Dropped in just by the skin of its teeth
Texas leaguer, but none the less.

So how was "Cotton Ed" to know
There'd be a hole in his bag of tricks.
"Who in the hell is 'Joltin' Joe!?"
Ed was the first of fifty-six!

New York again was the place to be
Joe shook his little town blues.
Twenty-two games was soon twenty-three
His message was trickling through.

Luck reared its head, the foibles of man
As thirty pulled into view.
"No error" said Dan, a Yankees fan
The headlines confirmed "Thirty-two!"

The Bronx came alive, Bo jangles danced
DiMaggio was now taking names.
Fans were caught by the seat of their pants
And his thirty-four one-hit games.

The next man to fall was Hornsby,
Though sadly ignored was Dahlen.
The end of the day dawned thirty-three...
Yet another man's record had fallen!

Sisler weighed in at forty-one
It stood, but the big man was through.
A last chance single off Anderson,
Joe's streak now screamed forty-two!

"He never did anything wrong on the field!"
So quick just not a base stealer.
His quest for the crown seemed so unreal,
On deck was Wee Willie Keeler!

Established in 1897
The streak, such a long time ago
Latest revision, see news at eleven
This Italian, DiMaggio.

For eighty-one years, forty-four withstood
A mark equaled only by Rose.
Twelve more games, now spelled out in wood
A legacy captured in prose.

Keltner robbed him with play after play
How could he have been so clever?
Hits just fell for Joe day after day
He wished it had gone on forever!

You could hear a pin drop on Broadway
No mortal could top it, it seemed.
To prove a point he got up the next day,
And prepared for another sixteen.

A storybook year was '41
Though heaven came calling for Lou
History played out under the sun
Dreams realized for a few.

Williams provided a .406 year
But surrendered to young number five
Now, it's the Yankee Clipper they cheer...
"The greatest Ballplayer alive!"

~ RWM

CHAPTER 13

~

A CASE FOR THIRD BASE

Voting for the Major Leagues first began in 1936 for the privilege of induction into the Baseball Hall of Fame. Since then, only thirteen third basemen have had the honor of seeing their bronze plaque hung in Monument Gallery for all eternity. Thirteen represents the fewest number of players enshrined of any of the positions in baseball. Why is this so? Any position referred to as "the hot corner" could be one explanation for such a small fraternity. Simply put, it is a very difficult position to play! The player must surely have two of the very things he is expected to catch! It's a position that demands of the player, the one sense that has allowed man to survive all these years on earth. Instinct! This is a luxury one can ill afford to neglect when the ball screams at you in moments measured in fractions of a second. To react instinctively, catch the ball and then make a strong and precise throw to first from one of the longer distances in the infield, takes a combination of guts and guile. Distinguished third basemen such as Sal Bando, Ken Boyer, Graig Nettles, Heinie Groh, Al Rosen, Terry Pendleton, Gary Gaetti, Tim Wallach and Buddy Bell to name just a few have, as yet been unable to make their way through the hallowed doors of the Hall of Fame. And with all due respect, probably never will. A good third-sacker is a rare commodity indeed, and finding one that can put up offensive numbers as well...well, that's another story all together. During Cal Ripken, Jr.'s Iron Man streak of consecutive games played at shortstop, no less than 34 different third basemen played beside him. According to Abbot and Costello, "I don't know" played third, and that pretty well sums it up for Ripken. I'm sure it was tough to keep track. One thing we do know for certain about these thirteen Hall of Famers is, although they played through many different eras in baseball history, they were the best third basemen of their time and all time. Each one of them deserves a spot within the walls of immortality.

Ray Dandridge

It will always be remembered, though not always mentioned, that two very fine players from the Negro Leagues have recently been inducted into the Hall of Fame and both were indeed third basemen. Ray Dandridge played with four different teams from 1933 to 1949 and was selected for the Hall by the Special Veteran's Committee in 1987. It was once said that a train could run through Dandridge's bow legs, but a baseball never did. In 1949 at age 35, he was signed by the New York Giants and batted .363 with their triple-A club in Minneapolis, as well as winning the American Association MVP award in 1950. His lifetime batting average was a robust .355. Despite his achievements, although Jackie Robinson had broken the color barrier in 1947, Dandridge never got the call from the Major League club. Willie Mays, who played with that same Minnesota team said, "Ray Dandridge helped me tremendously when I came through Minneapolis. Sometimes you just can't overlook those things. Ray was a part of me when I was coming along."

Judy Johnson

Judy Johnson was another third basemen who had played for four Negro League teams from 1921 to 1938. Although his given names were William Julius, he was often called Judy because he reminded everyone of the Chicago American Giant's player Judy Gans. (His given names were Robert

Edward, so why he was named Judy is anybody's guess.) His standout play at third reminded people of another future Hall of Famer, and he was often called the "black Pie Traynor." Johnson also handled the bat with a rare skill. He played in the first two Negro League World Series in 1924 and 1925, and led both teams in hitting in the Classic, with a .341 average. In 1929, Johnson reached a career high, hitting .401 with Hilldale, a team which later became the Darby Daisies. In 1932, he moved to the Pittsburgh Crawfords team where he played with Negro League greats, Josh Gibson (the black Babe Ruth), Oscar Charleston and Cool Papa Bell. This lineup was often compared to the New York Yankees "Murderer's Row." With the color barrier then broken after his retirement, Johnson scouted and coached for the Philadelphia Athletics from 1959 to 1973. The Committee on Negro Baseball Leagues voted him into the Hall of Fame in 1979. Unfortunately, the color barrier was a factor in the Major Leagues until 1947, but the Baseball Hall of Fame must be commended for finally honoring these two fine players. Their contributions to baseball will not be forgotten.

For the many current baseball fans that follow the game's past, the Dead Ball era was more than just what the name implies. It was a time in America that we can all look back on. We are now able to appreciate and delve into the illustrious history of the great ballplayers of that period. There are differing views it seems on the reason for calling the era by that particular name but I will contribute a few.

For the players who performed from 1900 to 1919, their approach to the game had changed, which inevitably influenced the statistics as well. The players of that era, for a better part of the game, used a dead or almost soft ball to play with mostly because they used the same ball for the entire game. Not only was the ball itself a detriment to the home run, but most ballparks were large, wide open fields. As if this wasn't enough to make problems for the hitter, spit-balls and other means of trickery had yet to be outlawed at this time. It was a pitcher's paradise in many ways and greats like Cy Young, Walter Johnson and Christy Matthewson were able to take advantage of these rules, or lack thereof, to some extent. The smart hitter's strategy was to take a heavy bat, choke way up on the handle, and learn not to be overly aggressive when attacking the ball. There are those who look back and say it was more than just the dead ball. Defense was more appreciated and keeping runs off the board was now almost as important as scoring them. Interestingly enough, stolen bases became more prevalent in the Dead Ball era than in any other.

Pitchers back then and nowadays as well seemed to perform more efficiently when a time frame or innings pitched during a game was not their main concern. Teams were using more pitchers in a game instead of the starter finishing the game. Fresh arms, fewer runs. What is also interesting was that a rule change took place which helped the man on the mound considerably. In those days, foul balls were not considered strikes (with the exception of the bunt) so any batter good with a stick could foul off balls all day long and not have it show up in the count. In 1901, the National League changed that rule as did the American League in 1903. Foul balls now would matter to the batter and count against him for the first two strikes just as it is in today's game.

Ty Cobb, Shoeless Joe Jackson and Honus Wagner were the best of their day and were extremely successful in the Dead Ball era. The League averages for teams tended to be low, while the League leaders still managed to maintain high averages. Dancers dance and good hitters hit! For example, in 1908, the National League average was .239, while Wagner topped the .354 mark. In 1910, while the League average was .243, Nap Lajoie enjoyed a .384 batting average. Despite all these obstacles and changes in the game, two third basemen, both future Hall of Famers, would be the cream that rose to the top during this era. Their outstanding hitting and stellar defense allowed them to shine, and their prowess on the field did not go unnoticed. The first was Jimmy Collins, who played from 1895 until 1908, and Frank "Home Run" Baker, who picked up where Collins left off in 1908, before finally calling it a day and hanging up his spikes after the 1922 season.

Jimmy Collins

James Joseph Collins was born January 16, 1870, in Buffalo, New York and died at the age of 73 on March 6, 1943. Collins revolutionized the position by becoming the first third basemen to play off the bag, as all third basemen do today, while some players still played the position with one foot on the bag. This enabled him to cut off balls hit to the right side of shortstop, while his athleticism allowed him to still grab balls hit down the line. He could chase down fly balls in shallow left field as well. He was the first to charge bunts and make bare-handed throws to first. As one sportswriter at the time wrote, he charged with "a swoop like a chicken-hawk." Very articulate. He joined Boston permanently in 1897 as an outfielder, but played in Louisville most of the two previous seasons as they were short of players. After Louisville third baseman, Walter Preston made four errors on four bunts while playing against the Baltimore Orioles, his manager John McCloskey suggested Collins try moving to third. The next four batters also tried to bunt. In Collins' own words, "McGraw bunted and I came in as fast as I dared, picked up the ball, and threw it underhanded to first base. He was out. Keeler tried it and I nailed him by a step. I had to throw out four bunters in a row before the Orioles quit bunting." He was now a third baseman with a defensive style all his own. Many copycats would quickly follow suit.

In 1898, Collins led the League in home runs with fourteen, and in 1903, played with Boston in the first modern World Series, beating the Pittsburgh Pirates five games to three. He batted .300 or better five times and finished his career with a .294 average, including 65 home runs, 983 RBI, and 194 stolen bases. As well as being an excellent contact hitter, he was a gentleman who felt compassion for his teammates and opponents alike. He once said, "I broke up four no-hit games and each time I felt like a heel." In 6,795 at bats, amazingly, he struck out only 32 times, averaging a paltry three K's per season. Completely unheard of in today's game. Jimmy Collins broke new ground and set the standard for today's players with an exclamation mark. He was voted into the Hall of Fame by the Veterans' Committee in 1945.

Frank (Home Run) Baker

John Franklin Baker was born in Trappe, Maryland, March 13, 1886, and died 77 years later, June 28, 1963, in the same town he was born in. During his thirteen-year Major League career, he stood out as the premier third baseman of his time, never playing an inning at any other position. He was a left-handed batter and joined Connie Mack's Philadelphia Athletics in 1908, remaining there as part of Mack's $100,000 infield until 1914. Mack had paid his infield the money but said he would never sell them for even close to that figure. The infield consisted of first baseman John McInnis, future Hall of Famer Eddie Collins at second, Jack Barry at shortstop, and Frank Baker at third. Connie Mack knew talent when he saw it and paid that talent accordingly. It paid off for him as well. Baker alone appeared in six World Series in his seven years in Philadelphia, hitting .363 in 25 games. It was during the 1911 World Series that Baker acquired his famous nickname. Fans nowadays chuckle at the thought that someone who had hit only 96 home runs in his whole career could seriously acquire such a moniker. That was the game in baseball's Dead Ball era. Baker, in fact, led the American League in home runs four years straight, from 1911 through 1914, when he tied Sam Crawford for the League lead with nine. Although he never hit more than twelve in any one season, as an everyday player from 1909 to 1919, no one hit more home runs than "Home Run" Baker. Only Ty Cobb collected more RBI during that period, and only Cobb, Tris Speaker and teammate Eddie Collins amassed more hits. In the 1911 World Series, he hit two memorable home run shots off two future Hall of Famers to solidify his namesake. In Game 2 against John McGraw's New York Giants, he hit a two-run homer off of Rube Marquard to win the game 3-1. In Game 3, he hit another home run to tie the game in the ninth inning off of Christy Matthewson, and his Athletics went on to win the game and the Series. The 52-ounce bat he used seems monstrous compared to the average 34-ounce bat used by players nowadays, but obviously it worked for him. In 1914, the Athletics were swept by the Braves and it would be an understatement to say the great Connie Mack was not amused. After the season Mack ridded himself of the entire team keeping only Baker. Realizing his worth, Frank embroiled himself in a contract dispute with the owner and chose to sit out the entire 1915 season in protest. Obviously a man of integrity. He was sold to the New York Yankees for the upcoming 1916 season. After his wife's untimely death, he again missed the 1920 season but returned in 1921 before finishing his career with the Yankees in 1922. After thirteen seasons, Baker wrapped up his career with a .307 average, 96 home runs, 987 RBI, and 235 stolen bases. He batted over .300 in five consecutive seasons from 1910 through 1914.

In 1920, a man by the name of George Herman Ruth joined the New York Yankees and hit 54 homers for them that same year. Frank Baker was able to watch the "Babe" up close for two years and the future of the game did not escape him. In November 1921, he had this to say about the "Bambino." "I hope he (Babe Ruth) lives to hit 100 home runs in a season. I wish him all the luck in the world. He has everybody else, including myself, hopelessly outclassed." Frank "Home Run" Baker was elected to the Hall of Fame in 1955 by the Veterans' Committee and enjoyed immortality until his death eight years later in 1963.

Pie Traynor

Harold Joseph Traynor was born in Framingham, Maine, on November 11, 1899, but for many baseball fans, he will forever be known as "Pie." Two theories surround the origins of his catchy nickname. His craving for pastries seems like the best fit for this likeable boy turned baseball Hall of Famer. It seems that when other youngsters would ask for ice cream after their sandlot games, young Harold would always ask for pie. Although this theory is the preferred one in most baseball circles, another began to make the rounds. As all young boys did at an early age, the young Traynor would return home covered in dirt after playing with friends all day. His father, being a printer, exclaimed one day that his boy resembled pied type, a term used in the industry. It's not as glamorous a theory as the first one; therefore history prefers to use the pastry reasoning. Whatever the origins, it seemed to fit, and would stay with him not only for his entire baseball career but throughout the rest of his life as well.

Pie Traynor began his Major League career with the Pittsburgh Pirates on September 15, 1920. He was brought in as a shortstop, but was soon moved to third base. He would spend more than a half century with the Pittsburgh organization serving as a player, manager, sportscaster and scout, and was warmly referred to as "Mr. Pirate." In seventeen years as a player and player/manager, he reached countless milestones and received numerous accolades from teammates and opponents. John McGraw considered him "the finest team player in the game." He batted over .300 an amazing ten times, and led the National League in put-outs a record seven times. Traynor never struck out more than 28 times in any one year, and remains among the Pirates all-time leaders in every category except home runs. (To put his strikeouts into perspective, the Major League leader at this time is Mark Reynolds who struck out a whopping 223 times in 2009.) Branch Rickey once stated "He was a mechanically perfect third baseman, a man of intellectual worth on the field of play."

In 1,864 games, all with Pittsburgh, Traynor collected 2,416 hits and along with his 58 home runs and 1,273 RBI, he achieved a lifetime batting average of .320. In Traynor's own words on playing the position he said, "Nobody taught me how to play third base...the way I learned was simply to tackle each situation as it arose and master it before moving on to something else. I think I learned more about playing third base in the morning bull sessions in the hotel lobby than I did out on the field."

As a player, he performed in two World Series, the first in 1925, when his Pirates beat the Washington Senators in seven games, and in 1927, where they were swept by the New York Yankees in four games. Traynor managed the Pittsburgh team for six seasons but was thought by some to be too gentle and thoughtful for the position. He once tried his hand as a reformer when, as manager, common sense told him to try and dissuade future Hall of Famer Paul Waner from hitting the bottle. He thought it was hurting not only Waner but the team. He told Waner, "Alcohol dulls the senses; you'd be a far greater hitter if you laid off the bottle. Will you do it for me?" Waner begrudgingly agreed, but his batting average soon dipped to a mere .241. One week later, Pie spoke to Waner once again, "Do me a favor, fall off the wagon." Apparently, Paul Waner never went to bed that night trying to catch up on lost time. The next day, he went to the ballpark and pounded out five hits. So much for reformation!

It is said Traynor never owned an automobile because he thought it would give him an excuse not to do one of the things he enjoyed most in life, which was walking. After his retirement, he became a radio sportscaster in Pittsburgh for many years. Friends say he would make the ten-mile round trip from his home on foot, never accepting a ride or giving a thought towards transit. In 1948, Harold Joseph Traynor was voted into the baseball Hall of Fame.

In 1969 as part of baseball's Centennial Celebration, he was named the greatest third baseman in baseball history. Three years later on March 16, 1972, Pie Traynor died of a respiratory ailment in Pittsburgh, Pennsylvania.

He is one of only nine Pirates (the tenth being Jackie Robinson's number 42) to have their number retired.

Freddie Lindstrom

Frederick Charles Lindstrom was born in Chicago on November 21, 1905 and passed away in that same Illinois town on October 4, 1981 at the age of 75. There are still some baseball hard-liners who argue about Lindstrom's validity as a Hall of Fame candidate. Although it's much too late to change anyone's mind, it's time for you to be the judge. Keep in mind the fact that even consideration in itself is cause for elation, but once again, the Hall is reserved for those very special ballplayers. If you have to stop and ponder a player's inclusion, then maybe he doesn't belong.

Most agree Freddie was a decent infielder, but not great. He joined the New York Giants farm club at sixteen years of age before becoming the youngest player to play in a World Series, joining the Major League club in 1924 at the tender age of 18. He hit .333 in that Series, collecting ten hits, four of which came off of future Hall of Famer Walter Johnson. The Giants lost that Series to the Washington Senators and it would be eleven long years before he would find himself in another Fall Classic. In 1935, his Chicago Cubs in the World Series once again, lost in six games. This time to Hank Greenberg and the Detroit Tigers.

A few followers of the sport say the only reason Lindstrom was voted into the Hall of Fame was because long-time friend Frankie Frisch ruled over the Veteran's Committee in the 1970s. Others think this point is grossly unfair. Lindstrom hit over .300 in seven different years, but led the League in hits only once, never leading in any other category. Although playing for four Major League clubs in his career, the New York Giants, Pittsburgh Pirates and Chicago Cubs, before retiring after the 1936 season with the Brooklyn Dodgers, he was an everyday player for only seven seasons. His two best years were 1928 when he hit .358, and 1930 when his average rose to .379. In 1928, he was runner-up to Jim Bottomley in the voting for National League MVP, and on June 25 of that same year, he recorded nine hits in a double-header, a mark that still stands today. In 1931, after moving to center field, he broke his leg and in 78 games hit an even 300.

In 1932, he slipped to .271 before being traded to Pittsburgh where he hit .310 and .290 in his two seasons there. The years of 1928 through 1930 are the only years Lindstrom played exclusively at third base, and played in only 48 games at that position after the 1930 season. In 1933 and 1934, he did not play third base at all.

In thirteen Major League seasons from 1924 to 1936, he compiled a .311 batting average while hitting 133 homers with 779 RBI and 84 stolen bases. Are these Hall of Fame numbers? The Veteran's Committee thought so and voted him in as a member in 1976. After his retirement in 1936, Lindstrom had his own radio sports program and managed a few years in the minor leagues before taking the coaching job at Northwestern University in 1947. The school is situated in Evanston, Illinois on the outskirts of his home town of Chicago, and he remained there for twelve years until 1960. Freddie Lindstrom is, and always will be, in the baseball Hall of Fame. He enjoyed that status for five years before his death in 1981.

George Kell

George Clyde Kell was born on August 23, 1922, in Swifton, Arkansas and would make his Major League debut 21 years later with the Philadelphia Athletics on September 28, 1943. Kell was by far the best player to emerge during the player shortages of WWII. He went on to play in fifteen American League seasons, playing for five different teams, and was a star third baseman well after the war had ended.

Kell started his career with Connie Mack's Athletics, and would go on to play with the Boston Red Sox, Chicago White Sox and the Baltimore Orioles. He enjoyed his finest years with the Detroit Tigers, having been traded there early in the 1946 season, anchoring that team until his trade to Boston in 1952. His strong arm and accurate throws enabled him to lead the League in assists four times, put-outs and double-plays twice, while leading the League in fielding percentage at third base seven different times. He batted over .300 nine times. Eight of them consecutive. He went on to play in ten All-Star games, again in eight consecutive years, missing only 1955 in that stretch. In 1948, Kell missed 57 games due to injuries after breaking his wrist on a pitch from the New York Yankees' Vic Raschi.

Several weeks later, he suffered a fractured jaw on a line drive off the bat of Joe DiMaggio. Damn Yankees! He still maintained a .304 average that year and bounced back to hit .343 in 1949, proving he was far from ball shy.

George Kell won the American League batting title in 1949, striking out only thirteen times for the entire year. It was the lowest total for any batting champ in history. What makes the title even more interesting was who he beat out for the honors. Ted Williams would go hitless in his last game of the 1949 season, and Kell went on to win the crown by less than two thousandths of a point. One of the closest races in baseball history. What made it incredibly worse for Williams was the fact that losing the batting title cost him his third Triple Crown. Only Rogers Hornsby in 1922 and 1925, and Williams in 1942 and 1947, had ever won it twice.

Kell retired after playing the 1957 season with the Baltimore Orioles and was succeeded at third base by none other than future Hall of Famer Brooks Robinson. Ironically, George Kell and Robinson were both voted into the Hall of Fame in the very same year, 1983. Brooks, with a 91.98 percent total and George by the Veteran's Committee. Although Kell played for five of the eight American League teams, he never once reached the postseason. He retired with a .969 fielding average, the highest in history at that time. A record which stood for twenty years. In 1,795 games, he accumulated 2,054 hits, 78 home runs, 870 RBI, 51 stolen bases and finished with a lifetime average of .306. Kell became the Detroit Tigers radio play-by-play man after his baseball career had ended and remained there for 38 years. Many of them alongside fellow Hall of Famer Al Kaline. Besides playing the game, George found another passion in the broadcast booth. After retiring once again in 1996, he often said that leaving his radio career was tougher than retiring from baseball.

Kell remained a loyal Tigers fan. He thought the players of today were far better than when he played. He once stated, "I played with (Hank) Greenberg and he hit it a long way. But there are ten Greenbergs out there now. That Alex Rodriguez, he might be the best player I've ever seen." George Kell died March 24, 2009 in Swifton, Arkansas. George Kell was also one of the very best of his day and any day!

Eddie Mathews

Edwin Lee Mathews was born in Texarkana, Texas on October 13, 1931, and moved with his family to Santa Barbara at the age of six. He remained in California until signing with the Boston Braves in 1949. He was drafted by nine different teams, but after much deliberation between him and his father, they chose Boston. The main reason was that hard-hitting third baseman Bob Elliot (the first third baseman ever to win an MVP award) was nearing the end of his career. Both Mathews' thought it would give Eddie a chance to play at his favorite position. Mathews signed with the Boston Braves as an 18 year old on the night of his high school graduation while still wearing his tuxedo. Baseball had strict rules about signing players before their graduation, so both parties agreed to wait until after midnight before signing.

In April 1952, Bob Elliot was traded to the New York Giants and Eddie Mathews began his Hall of Fame career. He hit 25 home runs in his rookie year before the Braves franchise moved to Milwaukee for the 1955 season. Mathews was the only player to play in all three cities in a Braves uniform after moving to Atlanta for the1966 season. He played in Milwaukee from 1953 to 1965, and after his one year in Atlanta, was traded to Houston for the 1967 season. Things didn't work out in Texas and he was again traded, this time to the Detroit Tigers for the remainder of 1967. He finished his career with a second World Series title in three tries while playing for Detroit in 1968, although he appeared in only two games, with three at-bats.

Mathews had a strong arm and played great defense, leading the League in assists three times, put-outs twice and at the time, was sixth among third baseman in double plays. But where he stood out among his peers was at the plate. After his rookie season in 1952, Eddie followed it up with 47 homers in 1953, dethroning the great Ralph Kiner for the home run title. Kiner had won the prestigious crown the previous seven years in a row. An amazing feat in itself! Mathews also had a powerful stroke and blinding bat speed. Brooklyn Dodgers pitcher Carl Erskine once said of him, "He swings the bat faster than anyone I ever saw. You think you've got a called strike past him and he hits it out of the catcher's glove."

Baseball fans had visions of a new Babe Ruth, as he hit 190 home runs in his first five seasons in the Major Leagues. Ty Cobb, never one to stroke another man's ego, once exclaimed, "I've only known 3 or 4 perfect swings in my time. This lad has one of them!" As a left-handed power-hitting third baseman, Mathews gave much of the credit for his success to his mom. "My mother used to pitch to me and my father would shag fly balls. If I hit one up the middle, close to my mother, I'd have some extra chores to do. My mother was instrumental in making me a pull-hitter."

His swing was showcased on the cover of the first Sports Illustrated in 1954, which turned out to be the first year Hank Aaron appeared alongside Mathews in a Milwaukee uniform. Together, along with Joe Adcock, and the pitching of Warren Spahn, Lew Burdette and Bob Buhl, they would battle the Dodgers for National League supremacy throughout the 1950s. In thirteen seasons together, Mathews and Aaron would combine to hit 863 home runs, the most in history for two teammates. It's no secret Eddie hit 512 career homers while Aaron went on to break Babe Ruth's all-time mark of 714, before finally finishing with a 755 total. When all was said and done, they accounted for an unbelievable 1,267 home runs altogether.

As mentioned earlier, Mathews played in three World Series, winning in 1968 with the Tigers after appearing in the Fall Classic in 1957 and 1958 with Milwaukee. The New York Yankees took the Braves to seven games in 1957, before finally losing to the Milwaukee powerhouse. Mathews was kept hitless in the first three games of the Series, but won Game 4 with a two-run home run off of Bob Grim in the tenth inning. He scored the only run in Game 5, giving Burdette a 1-0 win, and delivered a two-run double in Game 7, winning 5-0 for Burdette's third win of the Series. Mathews ended that game with a defensive gem, back-handing a drive off the bat of Bill Skowron with the bases loaded. The two teams would meet again in a seven-game Series in 1958, with the Braves losing this time to the team from New York. Mathews and Aaron made a formidable pair, with Hank batting third, and Eddie in the clean-up spot. He loved having Aaron batting in front of him. "If a pitcher got him out, he was so tired from the effort, he might make a mistake with me." Mistake or not, the two left many a pitcher feeling weak in the knees.

Despite his prowess at the plate, it was his competitiveness he was most proud of when looking back on his career. "I'd take on the other third baseman," he said. "I wanted to beat him in every department; fielding, hitting, running the bases. I played that game all my life and it kept me on my toes." Mathews played seventeen seasons in the Majors and in 2,391 games, finished with 512 home runs, 1,453 RBI and a .271 average. He topped the 100 RBI mark five times, led the National League in home runs twice, and walks in four separate years. Although he never received an MVP award, he was runner-up to Roy Campanella in 1953, and again finished second to Ernie Banks in 1959. He hit thirty or more home runs in nine straight years from 1953 to 1961. He was a nine-time All-Star, hitting forty or more home runs on four separate occasions, and on July 14, 1967, became just the seventh player in history to hit 500 homers. At the time of his retirement, he was tied with Ernie Banks for thirteenth on the all-time home run list.

Mathews turned to managing after his playing days were over and became involved in a minor controversy surrounding Aaron's pursuit of Babe Ruth's home run record. In his first at bat of the 1974 season, "Hammerin' Hank" tied the Babe's mark of 714 at Riverfront Stadium in Cincinnati. The Braves front office obviously wanted Aaron to break the record in Atlanta, in front of the home-field fans. Mathews decided to sit him out for the second game and planned to do the same for the third game before flying back home to Georgia. "Once he hit the tying home run," he said, "it was fair enough to sit him down." Baseball Commissioner Bowie Kuhn disagreed. As the rest of the world had also been doing, Kuhn was following Hank's quest very closely, and upon getting wind of Mathews' intentions, threatened him and the Atlanta organization with serious repercussions if they followed through with sitting him. Aaron then played the third game and ended up hitting number 715 in his first game back in Atlanta after all. Mathews began coaching the Braves late in the 1972 season, finishing fourth that year in the National LeagueWest. In 1973, he coasted to a fifth place finish and was eventually fired in July, 1974.

Despite his managerial record, Mathews should have been a lock for the Hall of Fame. Amazingly, it took five tries before finally receiving induction in 1978. A most deserved recognition but what took so long? He should have been a first ballot inductee. Eddie Mathews passed away February 18, 2001 in La Jolla, California after a battle with pneumonia. He was 69 years old.

As previously stated, baseball has provided us with extremely talented third basemen, worthy of their Hall of Fame status. Jimmy Collins revolutionized the "hot corner" with his innovative positioning and bare-handed fielding and Pie Traynor brought third base to a higher level of excellence in his day. Along with his fine defense, Eddie Mathews set new standards for offensive production, but on September 15, 1955, a young man by the name of Brooks Robinson made his debut for the Baltimore Orioles. He was brought in to fill the shoes of future Hall of Famer and recent retiree, George Kell, who had exhibited pride and grace on the field as well as off. Brooks Robinson would set the new standard on a defensive level by which all third baseman would forever be compared. He would prove himself to be a fine hitter during the regular season and a clutch performer during the playoffs as well. A player that could be relied upon to take his performance to another level, which he did over the course of his 39 post-season games and four World Series appearances. Over one 25-year period, the Orioles would have the best record in baseball, and it was no coincidence that Brooks Robinson played in 23 of those years.

Brooks Robinson

Brooks Calbert Robinson, Jr. was born on May 18, 1937 in Little Rock, Arkansas and would devote the better part of his life to the game of baseball. He made his first appearance in a Baltimore uniform at the age of 18, and would still be involved in the sport as president of the Major League Baseball Alumni Association until early into the 21st Century.

He was known as the "Human Vacuum Cleaner" or "Hoover" when he played, and held the game and the art of winning close to his heart. As ex-teammate and Hall of Famer Frank Robinson once said, "He was the best defensive player at any position. I used to stand in the outfield like a fan and watch him make play after play. I used to think WOW, I can't believe this." His aggressive play on the field belied his humble nature off it. He was well-respected by those around him and left an impression on everyone he came in contact with. Joe Falls of the Detroit News wrote of him, "How many interviews, how many questions, how many times you approached him and got only courtesy and decency in return. A true gentleman who never took himself seriously. I always had the idea he didn't know he was Brooks Robinson."

At the end of an outstanding career, he finished first in assists with 6,205, and put-outs with 2,697, while leading the American League in both categories eight times. He finished first in double plays with 618, and led the League in fielding eleven times, finally ending his career with a .971 percentage. It came as no surprise, that in 1983, in his first year of eligibility, he was voted into the Hall of Fame. At that time only the fourteenth player in history to accomplish that feat. As he explained in a 1999 interview, "I think it was my love for the game and passion for the game that got me into the Hall of Fame, not my talent." He was quick to add, "I go back every year to make sure they haven't taken my plaque off the wall though!"

In 2,896 games, he accumulated 2,848 hits along with 268 home runs and 1,357 RBI. He won an unbelievable 16 straight Gold Gloves from 1960 to 1975, and appeared in 18 consecutive All-Star games. Besides winning the American League MVP in 1964, Robinson would save his best performance for the 1970 World Series against Johnny Bench and the Cincinnati Reds. He took the Series MVP that year (the first one to ever take place on artificial turf), batting .429, but as the world would soon see, it was his glove that would make them stand up and take notice. He made several outstanding plays as the Orioles presided in five games over the Reds. Bench spoke to reporters after the game, "I will become a left-handed hitter to keep the ball away from that guy." Perhaps Baltimore broadcaster Rex Barney best summed up the Series Robinson had starred in, when he told reporters after the final game, "He's not at his locker yet, but four guys are over there interviewing his glove!"

It is mere speculation to say his offensive statistics alone would not have been enough to gain admittance to the Hall, but fortunately for Brooks and all baseball fans, the voters tend to look at all aspects of a player's career, including the integrity one brings upon himself and the sport. In his Hall of Fame interview in 1983, Brooks summed the game up this way: "Baseball is a game of memories. Every person you ever meet has a baseball memory. That's what baseball is all about, memories." Brooks Robinson gave us many of them! Gordon Beard summed up Robinson's career, not only for the fans of Baltimore, but baseball fans in general: "Brooks never asked anyone to name a candy bar after him. In Baltimore, people named their children after him."

What can you say about Mike Schmidt that hasn't been said or put into print, already? Most say, he is arguably, the best all-around third baseman to ever play the game. Others simply say, there is no argument, he is undoubtedly the best. To be compared defensively to Brooks Robinson, and to overpower Eddie Mathews offensively, is quite a statement in itself. Although Mike Schmidt's 12 All-Star selections and 10 Gold Gloves don't quite measure up to Robinson's 18 and 16 respectively, let's remember we are talking all-around third basemen here. In five less seasons, Schmidt had 268 more home runs than Brooks (over twice as many), and 238 more RBI. Regarding speed on the bases, there is no comparison. Schmidt was a smart baserunner, twice stealing more than 20 bases (23 and 29), and finished his career with 174 to Robinson's 28. Granted, they were two completely different ballplayers, but that's precisely the point. Mike Schmidt led his team to the postseason six times, winning two pennants and a World Series in 1980. He hit .381 in that Series, which won him the MVP, matching his National League MVP for that same year. The first of three MVPs for the Philadelphia slugger during regular season play.

Mike Schmidt

Michael Jack Schmidt was born on September 27, 1949, in Dayton, Ohio and in 1972, would make his debut with the Philadelphia Phillies, the team he would spend his entire 18-year career with. Major League success didn't come easy for Schmidt. In 1973, his first full season, he had the dubious honor of having the lowest batting average (.196) for any regular player. He did however give the fans a little taste of what was to come, hitting 18 home runs with 52 RBI.

The next year, with an off-season of hard work behind him, he returned with a .282 average, hitting 36 home runs and never looked back. "Anytime you think you have the game conquered," he said, "the game will turn around and punch you right in the nose." He never forgot his years of toiling in the Minor Leagues and put immense pressure on himself to perform at his utmost, day in and day out. Four years after retirement, before throwing out the first pitch of the 1993 World Series in Philadelphia, Mike reflected, "When I watch films of myself, I wish I had more fun playing. I wish I enjoyed myself more. But I was consumed with the pressure of trying to perform at a high level." That pressure molded him into the talented ballplayer he turned out to be, but the continued pressure also created a very intense player. This coupled with the fact that he played in the city of Philadelphia, where fans are simultaneously, the most knowledgeable, the most critical, and certainly one of the most vocal of any in baseball. Unfortunately, this made for a love-hate relationship which would last throughout his entire career. He summed up his situation with a smile: "Philly is the only city where you can experience the thrill of victory and the agony of reading about it the next day."

This need to perform on a daily basis was met head on with fans that were well aware of his abilities, his invaluable worth to the team and the city, as well as his contributions to winning, and made no bones about their daily expectations from him. These tumultuous years put a definite strain on their relationship. Schmidt once commented, "You're trying your hardest, you strike out and they boo. I act like it doesn't bother me, like I don't hear anything the fans say, but the truth is, I hear every word of it, and it kills me!"

Despite the obvious hardships, deep down it drove him to succeed. And succeed he did! One example of the man's strength came on June 10, 1974 at the Houston Astrodome. On perhaps one of the longest singles in baseball history, Schmidt connected on a pitch from Claude Osteen that hit a speaker hanging from the roof more than 320 feet away, and over 107 feet high. No one in their right mind, himself included, believed it could be, or had been done. Six years later, his 48 home runs would become the most ever by a third baseman. He in fact, failed to hit 30 or more homers in only three of his sixteen full seasons. In 2,404 games, Schmidt hit 548 home runs, and ironically, collected 1,595 RBI. This total would eventually leave himself, and another fine third baseman, George Brett, to whom comparisons would soon arise, in a first place tie for RBI at that position.

In another dash of irony, his .267 lifetime batting average had left him tied with his defensive contemporary, Brooks Robinson, for the lowest total for a Hall of Famer at third base. His keen eye at the plate allowed him to lead the National League in on-base percentage three times, and he won two legs of the coveted Triple Crown (HRs and RBIs) four separate times. In an eye-popping statistic, Mike Schmidt led the League in home run titles a total of eight times. A mark bettered only by the immortal Babe Ruth. In a not-so-glamorous statistic, his retirement left him with the third highest strike-out total in history, showing only that power numbers sometime come with a price! The Hall of Fame ignored this last statistic, and in 1995, opened its doors for him with a staggering 444 out of a possible 460 votes, for a 96.52 percentage.

Schmidt opted for a low profile after retirement and spent many days and early mornings with his other two passions, golf and fishing. He was talented enough at golf to try to win a card on the Senior Tour, and in 2001, he founded the Mike Schmidt Winner's Circle Offshore Invitational Fishing Tournament. However, this was not enough, and in 2003, he would finally face reality. "There's a bit of a void in my life. I've been involved in other things that have taken me away from baseball. The thing that would be most fulfilling is to get back into the game and life I know the most about." On October 14, he signed on to manage the Philadelphia farm team in Clearwater, Florida, with the hopes of one day finding himself with a Major League club. He spoke of his own work ethic, and we can only hope he can translate this to others: "If you could equate the amount of time and effort put in mentally and physically, into succeeding on the baseball field and measured it by the dirt on your uniform, mine would have been black."

Yogi Berra's son Dale, nicknamed Boo Boo for obvious reasons, spent parts of nine seasons at third base during an 11-year career in the Major Leagues. In a quote reminiscent of his father's gift for baseball eloquence, Dale gives us an insight into the difficulties of comparing players from different eras: "You can't compare me to my father. Our similarities are different." I'm sure a few eyebrows were raised at that statement, but it does help us in explaining why, whenever the question of who was the best at any position arises, it will most likely be preceded by the word, arguably! Such is the case for the next third baseman, and perhaps the best ever at his position to be enshrined into the Hall of Fame.

George Brett

George Howard Brett was born on May 15, 1953, in Glen Dale, W. Virginia. Those who played with him, those who played against him, the many millions who watched him light up the playing field with his brilliance, or the countless fans of the future who will only read about his career or watch his many highlight reels, will all rise up to agree on one point: George Brett is arguably the best third baseman to ever play the game! Obviously that is my personal opinion, but sound arguments will always be made for others to top the list. So again I say, arguably. These words are not written to sway your opinion, nor are they a blatant attempt to make up your mind for you, but to simply point out why so many of us think of George Brett in this regard. As a young player coming up and throughout most of his playing career, he somehow remained a bachelor. His good looks and baseball savvy certainly made him one of the most enviable players in any sport. His statistics alone show an amazing young man, who despite a few injuries, made the most of his God-given talents. His hard work on the field, and the respect he garnered from those around him, made him a living legend, and one for the ages. He is widely regarded throughout the baseball world as the finest clutch hitter to ever grace the field. The intended absence of the word arguably on this point speaks volumes. I know a lot of Red Sox fans will bring up the name David Ortiz at this point, but George is still the man. The Kansas City Royals' General Manager (1982-1990) John Scherholz, once said of him, "George Brett could fall out of bed on Christmas morning and hit a line drive." Most who followed his career fully believe that fine compliment.

Brett's Minor League statistics were obviously good enough for him to be summoned to the Majors, but they gave no indication as to the kind of player he would turn out to be. In three plus seasons in the Minors, he hit an adequate .281, but in his second pro season also led the California League in errors for a third baseman. In his first Major League call-up, he hit a paltry .125, and in his first full season with Kansas City in 1974, he managed only two home runs with 47 RBI. Batting coach Charlie Lau, however, liked the potential he saw in this young man and took him under his wing. Lau taught him to hit the ball to all fields with every type of pitch instead of sitting on the fast ball. Brett listened intently, and the lessons were readily adapted. In his second full season, he led the League in hits and triples, while raising his batting average to an impressive .308. He was on his way! He even changed his uniform number and soon began to wear number five in honor of his hero, Brooks Robinson. The rest, as they say, is history. He would remain in a Royals uniform for his entire 21 seasons, spanning 1973 through to 1993, and played in an incredible 2,707 games. He performed in eleven consecutive All-Star games, thirteen in total, with a batting average of exactly .300. The bigger the show, the more George Brett showed!

George was a menace to every pitcher he came up against. The opposing managers fared no better, and came apart at the seams trying to figure out how to pitch to this guy. With the game on the line, both teams knew the batter Kansas City wanted at the plate was none other than George Brett. The late Sparky Anderson, one of the great managers of all time, had this to say on the subject: "I've always loved the way he played the game of baseball, and I always thought he was the most dangerous hitter I ever faced – certainly in the American League. Back with Cincinnati, I used to walk the Giants' Willie McCovey all the time because he could just kill you. I thought I'd never treat another hitter that way, but I wound up doing it with George."

In 1979, Brett accumulated 85 extra-base hits and became only the sixth player ever to collect 20 or more doubles, triples and home runs in the same year (Willie Mays had been the last). Obviously it was quite a feat, but no one could have guessed that 1979 would be a precursor to one of the most amazing years for any batter in baseball history.

George Brett never failed to amaze. Every year sparkled with new expectations and possibilities, and George rarely disappointed. He became the only player in history to win batting titles in three different decades. His first title in 1976, in only his third full season, came down to the last day, in a battle with teammate Hal McRae and future Hall of Famer, Rod Carew. Although there was some minor controversy involved, (McRae accused the opposing team of letting a base hit drop in so George could win the crown) both players later admitted that Brett had deserved to win. In 1990, at the age of 37, his last title enabled him to become the third oldest player to win a batting crown, younger than only Ted Williams and Honus Wagner. Elite company no doubt! (Brett's other batting title came in 1980).

There are numerous instances in Brett's career that stand out and many more that bring with it a cause for endearment. The constant reminder of his hemorrhoid problem in the 1980 World Series sticks out (for lack of a better word) as one instance, and what we simply refer to as "the pine tar incident" with Billy Martin and the Yankees would be another. But perhaps his crowning achievement came with winning his batting title in 1980. Not since Ted Williams had delivered a .406 average in 1941, had anyone seriously threatened the .400 mark, but by June of that year, Brett had sent the message that he would be the next contender. As late as May 22, he was stuck on a .255 average. Baseball fans knew to expect better things from him, but George far exceeded all expectations and hit .427 from that point on. He batted a sizzling .472 for the month of June and followed that up with a mind-boggling .494 for the month of July. As the third week of August arrived, Brett, with five hits in Milwaukee, reached his highest point of the year with a .407 average. He finished August at a .430 clip for the month and was still over the .400 mark well into the first week of September when nagging injuries began to nip at him. If not for a thumb and wrist injury, which undoubtedly hampered his swing, the feat would have surely been accomplished. He fell five hits short and finished the year at .390, the highest mark since 1941 and the highest total for a third baseman in the 20th Century. For the entire season, Brett also hit .466 with runners in scoring position. The highest mark ever recorded since the inception of this statistic.

Brett once said of himself, "If I stay healthy, I have a chance to collect 3,000 hits and 1,000 errors." Although he fell only 708 errors short of his prediction, he did in fact, collect 3,154 hits, along with 317 home runs and as previously mentioned, tied Mike Schmidt for first place in RBI for a third baseman, with 1,595. His 665 doubles, 137 triples and 201 stolen bases are a testament to not only his speed, but his heads up, aggressive base running.

In 1980, he won the American League MVP and collected the Sporting News' Player of the Year Award for his fine season. The Royals made it to the World Series that same year but despite Brett's .375 batting average, his team fell to Schmidt's Philadelphia Phillies in six games. Losing didn't sit well with Brett at any time as this quote reveals, "If a tie is like kissing your sister, losing is like kissing your grandmother with her teeth out." He returned to the Fall Classic again in 1985, batting a mere .370, while leading his team to a seven-game victory over the St. Louis Cardinals. In addition to his two World Series appearances, Brett also led his team to six American League Championship Series, where he hit .340 in 27 games, with 35 hits and 9 home runs. His Hall of Fame plaque is hardly stretching the truth as it reads in part "...a clutch hitter whose profound respect for the game led to universal reverence."

In 1983, George was the central figure in the previously mentioned "pine tar incident" which became one of the most controversial events in baseball's long history. The Royals were in Yankee Stadium on July 24, down 4-3 with two out and one on in the ninth inning, when Brett came to the plate to face "Goose" Gossage. These two were no strangers to each other, Brett having hit a seventh inning upper-deck home run off Gossage in the third game of a three-game sweep to put Kansas City into the 1980 World Series. This game was no different as Brett connected once again to give the Royals a 5-4 lead. No sooner had Brett circled the bases, than he witnessed Yankee skipper Billy Martin approaching home plate umpire Tim McClelland. After a short conference at the plate, McClelland asked to see Brett's bat, which, with George, was now in the Kansas City dugout. No one was more curious than George as the entire stadium wondered what Martin was up to. As Billy watched the umpires confer he was heard to tell McCellend "You gotta call him out, pal." Some say Yankee bench coach Don Zimmer called the rule to Martin's attention, while others attribute the cleverness to Yankee third baseman, Graig Nettles. Regardless, seconds later, McClelland, (citing Rule 1.10(b) which states "a bat may not be covered by such a substance more than 18" from the tip of the handle") looked toward the Royals dugout, raised his arm and signaled Brett out.

Brett at once came flying out of the dugout, all arms and legs, in a direct charge towards home plate umpire McClelland. It took several teammates and Kansas City manager Dick Howser to restrain Brett and he was eventually thrown from the game. What a turnaround! The umpire ruled that "heavy pine tar reached 19-20 inches from the tip of the handle, and lighter pine tar reached another 3 or 4 inches." Despite Brett and Howser's protests, the home run was wiped off the Board and the Yankees went on to win the game 4-3.

A nationwide stir erupted and debates began from one corner of the country to the other. Howser's protest was put to American League president Lee McPhail, and after much pressure and deliberation, he ruled in favor of Brett and re-instated the homer. The next time the teams met, the game was resumed with two out in the top of the ninth, Royals leading 5-4, a score which, at long last turned out to be the final. McPhail's statement revealed the League's position that "games should be won and lost on the playing field – not through technicalities of the rules." And so ended another chapter in baseball's sometimes strange past. Brett had been vindicated!

As Lee McPhail's statement in part and more importantly declared "in the spirit of the rules," so had George Brett's career also taken that same path. His enthusiasm for the game in which he excelled, paid the highest of dividends for him when his playing time had finally come to an end. It seems fitting that in the final game of the 1993 season in Texas, he made a grand exit with a base hit up the middle in his last at bat. His respect for the game was boldly pronounced as he commented on the most difficult decision he would make in the sport he loved. "I could have played one more year but, if I'd played one more year, I'd have played for the money, and the game didn't deserve that." After the 1993 season, Brett moved to the front office as the Kansas City Royals Vice President in charge of baseball operations. In the early 1980s, George had been awarded a lifetime contract from the Royals, and remains with the Kansas City organization to this day.

To say George Brett retired with impressive statistics would be a drastic understatement, but to make a final point, he is the only player in history to amass 3,000 hits, 300 home runs, 600 doubles, 100 triples and 200 stolen bases. In 1999 the Hall of Fame Voting Committee presented their tally and Brett was a shoo-in, receiving 488 out of a possible 497 votes for a 98.19 percentage. This mark was the fourth highest in history at the time, trailing only Ty Cobb, Tom Seaver, and fellow inductee of that same year, Nolan Ryan. Long-time Royals broadcaster Fred White, perhaps put George Brett in the proper perspective when he so historically stated, "I think when George goes to heaven, there will be the Babe, and Gehrig and a few of the really, really great ones all hanging around together, and one of 'em will say 'Hey, that's George Brett!'" History has spoken! George Brett is arguably the best third baseman to ever play the game!

Over the years, there have been heated discussions whether to have Ron Santo ushered through the doors in Cooperstown. Of course Chicago Cubs fans were at the front door in these debates. His impressive statistics and stellar defensive play definitely put him up for consideration, but were they enough for him to be enshrined? What many of us overlook is that at the time of his retirement, for third basemen he was sixth all-time in putouts with 1,930 and ninth in fielding percentage at .954. His detractors will ask the question, why then in 1980, his first year of eligibility, was he only mentioned on 4 percent of the ballots cast by the Baseball Writers Association of America (BBWAA)? A ridiculously low number and one that as a result would have his name removed from future voting. Over the years and across the country, fans were upset and of the opinion that some of their heroes and great ballplayers were being left out in the cold. Santo was one of many players who benefited and was reinstated to the voting process for another fifteen years. He received 13 percent of the vote in 1985 and in his last year of eligibility in 1998, he was still short of induction at 43 percent. (75 percent is needed for induction) Doors were opened and opportunities arose for veteran players who had been retired for more than twenty years. Rule changes for the Veterans Committee allowed voting to continue and from 2003 to 2009, the Chicago Cubs third baseman still came up short of the votes needed. Don't get me wrong, Ron Santo was obviously a fine third baseman, but there seems to be some discrepancy over his status of inclusion. All those years of eligibility and coming up well short year after year begs us to ask this important question. Does he really belong with the elite players in baseball history? Because that is what we are talking about. I'm sure at least 99 percent of the players that reach the Major Leagues are obviously good ballplayers, but the Hall of Fame is for the best of the best, with no questions asked. Was he as highly regarded outside of Chicago as he was in the Windy City? There are many other inductees that raise eyebrows as well but we are talking about third base here. The brilliant and groundbreaking statistician Bill James backed Santo's induction to the Hall and believed he was one of the top 100 players of all time and had him ranked sixth among third basemen. You can't argue about James' credentials and he is a good man to have on your side. After many years and dozens of baseball books, the Boston Red Sox, in 2003, hired him as an analyst and for his incredible insight. After a ghastly drought of World Series wins, it's somewhat ironic that Bill James and the Red Sox Nation have celebrated wins in 2004, 2007 as well as their recent 2013 Series victory. Coincidence? Baseball is all about statistics and Bill James is the King.

Once again, the voters, after so many years of passive exclusion, decided to finally honor Ron Santo and have his plaque hung with pride. For some, the discussion will remain but the decision has been made. A new 16-member Golden Era Committee formed in 2011 decided he should be granted status and he was finally inducted into The Baseball Hall of Fame in 2012. Unfortunately, Santo died on December 3, 2010 and sadly would never know of his impending and long awaited inclusion alongside the games' elite. His wife Vicky gave a heartfelt and gracious speech on his induction day and at long last, a long overdue congratulations goes out to Ron Santo and his family.

Ron Santo

Ronald Edward Santo was born on February 25, 1940, in Seattle, Washington. He was quoted in the Chicago Tribune in a 1992 interview about his early days: "As long as I can remember, I had a glove in my hand. (My Dad) was the first person to put a glove in my hand when I was two years old, and you could say he was the one who started me in baseball..." Ron was signed right out of high school as a free agent by the Chicago Cubs and made his debut on June 26, 1960. Ron always had many fans and admirers, and whether on the field or in the broadcast booth, always wore his heart on his sleeve. In one of his more famous quotes, he laid testament to that fact: "You can have all the talent in the world, it's not gonna get you through...it's what you have in your heart." Fortunately for the Cubs and fans of the game, he had both.

In 1962, he led the National League in assists for the first time with 332 and continued to lead the National League in assists in consecutive years through to 1968. Although he never came close to Cal Ripken's streak (who has?), he was a bit of an iron man himself playing in every game in 1961, 1962, 1963, 1965 and 1968. He averaged an amazing 105 RBI from 1963 through 1970 and had four straight 30 HR years starting in 1964. Throw in the nine All-Star appearances and you have what many believe was a Hall of Fame career. To show his heart was always in the right place, a few years after retirement in 1974, Ron decided to work closely with the Juvenile Diabetes Research Foundation and formed his own Ron Santo Walk to Cure Diabetes in the city he so loved. Until his death in 2010, he helped to raise $65 million for the cause.

Ron Santo battled diabetes his whole life and eventually lost both legs to the disease within a year of each other. Today, after years of research, modern advances in the medical field, for the most part, allow us to control diabetes with medication and diet but that was not the case when Santo began his career in the early 1960s. He tried to keep his situation quiet in the early years and to those who took notice, he could often be seen eating a candy bar which, unbeknownst to many, boosted his blood sugar levels whenever he felt the need. He was careful to guard his secret as he thought it might cost him his job and career; a secret he finally announced to the baseball world on his own appreciation day in 1971.

In 1966, Santo had his cheekbone fractured from a pitch thrown by New York Mets pitcher Jack Fisher. Ron did not play for a couple of weeks but on his return, became the first player to wear a batting helmet with a protective ear flap, the same helmets we still see today's players wearing.

In a June 1969 game, after the Cubs had scored four runs in the bottom of the ninth inning, Santo, for some happy reason, jumped up and down and began clicking his heels. After the game, manager Leo Durocher asked Santo to continue this feat, perhaps for the good luck it might bring, and he did. After each home win, Santo could be seen clicking his heels, which not only aggravated the opposing team, but also provided motivation to beat the Cubs and their apparent arrogance. He continued doing this until September 2, 1969, as the clicking brought with it too much controversy. They were in first place as of that date but lost seventeen of their last twenty-five games. The "Miracle Mets" stormed through their final fifty games and eventually won the World Series that memorable year.

After the Major Leagues of Baseball finally agreed to go back to work after the 1972 strike, one of the agreements announced was a new 10 and 5 Rule. It meant that a player with ten years of Major League seniority, and in his last five consecutive years with the same club could veto any trade he didn't agree with. Ron Santo became the very first player to use that rule to his advantage after the Cubs had agreed to a deal with the California Angels in 1973. He was very happy and quite settled in Chicago, so the following year, taking that into consideration, the Cubs moved Santo across town to the White Sox. The "South Siders" already had a fine third baseman by the name of Bill Melton. Santo had no choice but to become the new DH, which he disliked immensely. He still wanted to play the game but ended up retiring after the 1974 season at the very early age of 34.

President Andy MacPhail said in part about Ron Santo: "...very few players are as closely connected with the franchise as Ron Santo is with the Chicago Cubs." Ron Santo's Chicago Cubs jersey bearing the number 10 was retired by the National League club and now hangs at Wrigley Field along with former teammates Billy Williams (26) and Hall of Famer Ernie Banks (14).

Looking back over Ron Santo's career, his statistics were incredibly impressive. He finished his career with 342 home runs, 2,254 hits, 1,331 RBI, 1,138 runs scored and compiled a .277 batting average in 8,143 at bats.

Ron Santo died December 3, 2010, in Scottsdale, Arizona at 12:40 A.M. of complications from bladder cancer and diabetes. Unfortunately, he would never know about his impending and long-awaited induction into the Baseball Hall of Fame. W.G. Radio Broadcast partner Pat Hughes had this to say about his friend and colleague at his memorial service: "...the two things he loved more than anything in his life were his family and the Chicago Cubs."

On the day Ron Santo was enshrined in the Hall of Fame, the starting nine in the lineup for the Cubs that day all jumped and clicked their heels as they ran out onto the ball field. An obvious salute to a great baseball player and Chicago Cub. A statue of Ron Santo stands in tribute outside Wrigley Field.

Granted, there are ballplayers with more or less impressive statistics, but a contribution to winning is also very important in the minds of the Committee. Playoff performances and World Series appearances also play a large part in the selection process. Under careful scrutiny, I think we would all have to admit, there are players in the Hall of Fame that perhaps don't deserve to be there, and whatever avenues were traveled to include them should be looked at for future players. Should good ballplayers be inducted just because someone else was inducted? So and so is in the Hall, so if he is, then this player should be also? I don't think so! Not exactly a stand-up argument but that seems to be where we are headed.

Surely we would all like to see our favorite players inducted and if you have ever been to Cooperstown, it is a great place to watch the ceremonies. Major League Baseball has many supporters worldwide, but we should all take the time to support the Hall of Fame as well. They continue to make any visit a fascinating adventure and classy one as well. The staff is not only incredibly knowledgeable but accessible and approachable. A definite highlight in the lifetime of even the mildest of fans. The doors are open to you twelve months of the year so do take advantage.

Wade Boggs

Wade Anthony Boggs was born June 15, 1958, in Omaha, Nebraska, but did his growing up in Tampa, Florida. In 1976, he graduated from Plant High School and his outstanding play in the sport caught the eye of many baseball fans. One of those fans happened to be the Boston Red Sox, who drafted him that very same year in the seventh round of the Amateur Draft. Perhaps they knew what they were getting when they signed him, perhaps not, but who would ever think at that time they had a future Hall of Famer on their hands. The talent, potential and expectations of young players can be so up and down if not downright quirky. What an understatement! If only they knew.

Most baseball players are overly superstitious, probably the most of any sport, but Boggs was perhaps over the top. He seemed infatuated by the number 17. Besides getting up at the same time every day, he was in the batting cage taking his swings at precisely 5:17, did his running at 7:17 every day and had to take 117 ground balls for infield practice. The path he took to his position at third base had to be the same every inning. But perhaps the one superstition he was most famous for was his penchant for a chicken dinner before each and every game. The man Hall of Famer Jim Rice dubbed "Chicken Man" had to have chicken fried, baked, sautéed, or any which way before he took the field. It seems only fitting that he had to have his own cookbook with varied chicken dishes entitled, what else but, "Fowl Tips: My Favorite Chicken Recipes".

In 1976, his first Minor League season, after hitting .263 in Elmira N.Y., Boggs never once hit below .300 in his next five Minor League seasons. In fact, his last year in the Minors, 1981, Boggs hit a convincing .335 for Pawtucket, his Triple-A club in Rhode Island, making it a much easier decision for the Boston Red Sox to finally come calling. Also, in that very same year, his Pawtucket Red Sox played an unheard of 33 inning baseball game, which would turn out to be the longest game in professional baseball history. The game began on Saturday, April 18, at approximately 8:30 in the evening as Boggs and his Red Sox played against another future Hall of Fame player and his Rochester Red Wings. This player's name happened to be Cal Ripken, Jr. The teams played until 4:07 a.m., where after 32 innings, with the score deadlocked at 2-2, the players were completely spent and totally exhausted. The game resumed on Tuesday, June 23 and took all of eighteen minutes for the Red Sox to score in the bottom of the 33rd inning. In total, the game lasted an amazing eight hours and twenty-five minutes. Wade Boggs had four hits. Players from both teams signed a baseball that was sent to the Hall of Fame in Cooperstown, New York. A 25-year reunion was held in 2006 in Providence, Rhode Island.

Wade Boggs' fine play in Boston catapulted him into the baseball limelight. In his eleven years in Boston, from 1982 to 1992, Boggs would explode into baseball and Red Sox history. His first batting title came in 1983 when he lit up the baseball diamond with a .361 average. After slumping in 1984 where he could only muster a mere .325 average, he rattled off four straight batting titles from 1985 to 1988, batting .368, .357, .363 and .366 respectively. He also collected 431 walks and 861 hits in those four seasons alone. A pure hitter! As he said himself, "I didn't get over 1300 walks without knowing the strike zone." Boggs also had seven straight years that he was able to rattle off 200 or more hits. An American League record he held until Ichiro Suzuki batted his way to ten straight years. He played with many great ballplayers in his years with Boston as evidenced by their 1986 World Series appearance. The Red Sox thought they had it won in Game 6 that year, but I'll let Bill Buckner finish that story.

It was during those years in Boston that he struck up a friendship with another Red Sox alumni, Ted Williams. The two would form a great bond. Although fishing was their passion, we can only imagine what words were spoken about the art of hitting.

Throughout his entire career, Boggs only batted under the magic .300 number a mere three times. Unfortunately, one of those years was 1992 when he somehow squeaked out a .259 average which made it easier for both parties in his split from Boston. Two of baseball's storied franchises, the Yankees and Dodgers doggedly pursued his services. The Bronx

Bombers finally scooped their man by agreeing to add another year to his contract over the two that L.A. had offered.

It turned out to be another great move for the Yanks as Boggs rewarded not only them, but himself with three exceptional years, both offensively and defensively. He spent a total of five years in New York and had three straight trips to the All-Star game and four seasons in which he again batted over .300. New York seemed to bring out the best in him. Not only was his bat still on fire but he was extremely proud of his two Gold Glove Awards which came in 1994 and 1995.

Statistics and achievements are always nice to look back on after retirement, but especially so when the Hall of Fame comes calling. Boggs finally claimed the ultimate personal goal he had chased for so many years when he helped the Yankees capture their first World Series title in eighteen long years. It would be his first and only, but oh so sweet!

Time has a way of catching up to most of us and after a 1997 season, which brought about only his second season hitting below .300 (.292), in only 353 at bats, the writing was on the wall. It's to Boggs' credit that batting .292 signifies an off year for him but it was finally time to go home where it all began 22 years before. Home to Florida and the new franchise in Tampa Bay.

Boggs signed on for what was to be his last two years of Major League Baseball with a brand new team not only for him, but for Tampa as well. The Devil Rays (it has since been shortened to the Rays) played their very first game in team history on March 31, 1998 against the Detroit Tigers. As fate would have it, the homecoming was complete as Boggs hit the very first home run in the young team's history in the bottom of the sixth inning of an eventual 11-6 loss.

On August 7, the very next year, Boggs became at the time, the only player in Major League Baseball history to hit a home run for his 3,000th hit (in 2011, Derek Jeter would become the second player to do so; Alex Rodriguez would also homer for his 3000th hit in 2015). Boggs would go on to collect only ten more hits that year and wrapped up a storied career on August 27th with 3,010 hits. On April 7, 2000, Wade Boggs' number 12 was retired by the Tampa Bay Devil Rays.

A few years ago, Boggs became part of a team called "Go the Distance Baseball". For a cool $3.4 million, this team bought the cornfield and baseball field (with farmhouse and all) used in the Academy Award nominated movie "Field of Dreams" located in Dyersville, Iowa. Included in their "Dream" project is a vision to build twenty-four baseball diamonds, a training center, club houses and accommodations. The first phase is thought to be ready around the middle of 2014. It seems a shame to have to commercialize this sacred ground to such an extent but if this agreement had not gone through, these fields might have just been swallowed up by the surrounding landscape. This step forward is quite commendable. Of this investment, Boggs would say "...I had goose bumps. It tears you up a little bit. It's emotional. I mean, it's everything that everybody dreams of. It's playing with your dad in your backyard."

If there was any lingering doubt about Wade Boggs inclusion in the Hall of Fame, perhaps we should go over the facts. He appeared in twelve consecutive All-Star games (behind only George Brett and Brooks Robinson for third baseman); he won five batting titles and eight Silver Slugger awards. And if this wasn't enough, his four straight batting titles puts him once again in elite company, as Tony Gwynn, Ty Cobb, Rogers Hornsby and Rod Carew are the only players to achieve that feat. Boggs and Gwynn both hit over .350 in four straight seasons as well, making them the only players since 1931 to reach that milestone. Boggs and Gwynn, together again, joined Rod Carew and Lou Brock in a somewhat unique statistic. They became the only four players in post-World War II history to have at least 3,000 hits while compiling less than 160 home runs.

In his Hall of Fame induction speech on July 31, 2005, Boggs had these words of advice and encouragement for future Little Leaguers and perhaps Hall of Famers: "...life is about obstacles, endeavors in life are not to be overlooked. Our lives are not determined by what happens to us but how we react to what happens, not by what life brings us but the attitude we bring to life. A positive attitude causes a chain reaction of positive thoughts, events and outcomes. It is a catalyst and it sparks extraordinary results..."

For most baseball fans and critics, Wade Boggs was an obvious choice for induction as the 91.9 percent voting result attests to. In eighteen Major League seasons, he played in a total of 2,440 games garnering 9,180 at bats and along the way managed 1,014 RBI. Not bad for a man who was a leadoff hitter for a good portion of his career. As he said himself: "...my job was to get on base to score runs. I was Billyball before Billyball. I got on base 300 times a year." His 3,010 hits and life-time batting average of .328 didn't mar his credentials either, but some voters and a great many fans didn't like the fact that he hit only 118 homers, or the fact that he was not a standout player defensively. Shouldn't it be about all-round play at your chosen position? But, he did finally win two Gold Gloves with the Yankees (thanks to Clete Boyer) and Ty Cobb only hit 117 home runs. (I know Cobb also had 1,179 more hits but he also played six more years). Maybe Boggs' crazy desire for chicken every day rubbed some people the wrong way, or family men might not like the fact that he made a mockery of his marriage by apparently having one too many girlfriends lined up on road trips. Late-night talk show host David Letterman couldn't resist this poke at Boggs when the news of that little tidbit broke. "According to The Sporting News, over the last four years, Wade Boggs hit .800 with women in scoring position." The Voting Committee ignored this last statistic and put Boggs in the Baseball Hall of Fame where he undoubtedly belongs.

There is obviously an enormous mountain of criteria involved that make each selection to the Hall either possible, improbable, or a fact. Did he play enough games? Did he make too many errors? Maybe he never made it to the postseason or didn't hit enough home runs. Maybe he wasn't a big-game player, wasn't a team player, or maybe he just rubbed some people the wrong way! Pete Rose is a perfect example of that reasoning. Gambling is a serious crime in baseball and should be dealt with and it has been. The recent steroid situation has put a stain on the sport and again, in my humble opinion, these players should be held accountable for their actions. But will an apology be enough for someone like Pete Rose to finally reach his dream? Some think it's his arrogance that keeps him out of Cooperstown. If stats alone were enough, Pete Rose should be exalted and carried in on the writers' shoulders. Head first! Call it the "human factor," but it's the right of the voters to call it as they see fit. I agree with that process and continue to abide by it though not always happily.

Some years ago, Alex Rodriguez moved to the New York Yankees and the third base position. He seems destined to be the next one enshrined once his career finally comes to an end. Until recently! That event is now clouded in uncertainty as all the sports world is more than aware of. Without a doubt the voters will take into consideration the harm inflicted on the game and its impressionable youth, in regards to his alleged use of steroids and the apparent absence of truth surrounding this unfortunate incident. He had already established himself in the game with an amazing 345 home runs while playing ten years at shortstop with stopovers in Seattle and Texas, but I'm sure he would have wanted the NY on his hat in the now highly unlikely event that his face is ever sculpted in bronze. As of 2015, Alex Rodriguez has since returned to baseball and the New York Yankees. As of this writing, his one-year suspension, apparently far behind him, A-Rod is in the midst of a highly successful comeback. How long will it last, only history will tell.

At times, putting these players and their place in history into the proper perspective can be a long and arduous task. Maybe a player stands out because of a preferred era, or perhaps he plays for a favorite team. Maybe just one feat he performed endears us, or a certain talent he possessed. Do all the third basemen mentioned here deserve immortality? The voters thought so, and in the Hall of Fame, they shall remain forever.

Does one third baseman figure prominently in your thoughts? One thing is for certain, all the men who played the "hot corner" mentioned here, as well as countless others who toiled at their position, brought something unique, sometimes historical, and most often the whole package to the playing field. They have all left their mark on the game and will be remembered for doing so by baseball fans for many years to come. Deservedly or not, the voting is not left in the hands of the players. Voters vote and the players play. Let's leave them to it!

In closing, I have to say that personally speaking, if any fan with considerable knowledge of the game has to stop and consider whether a player deserves the ultimate commemoration for his life's work in the game, which is induction into the Hall of Fame, then he doesn't belong. Cooperstown is reserved for the elite. Period!

~

A THIRD'S EYE VIEW

My left hand holds a wealth of gold gloves, the other a grip on pure thunder
I was blessed with a gun, some guts and the guile for throwing out base-runners.
I was born with an instinct for timing and tact, soft hands to cradle the catch
My life played out on a bed of green grass, and a powder blue sky to match.

Consumed with flare and a confident stride, my cannon rears back and let's fly
The hopeful runner is swiftly gunned down, in the blink of an umpire's eye.
A tip of the hat to acknowledge the crowd, an attempt to swallow the sound
A routine toss from the rookie at short, relayed to the man on the mound.

A shift to the right to guard the white line, with a pull-hitter due up next
Not a moment to daydream or wonder, or anticipate the slugger on deck!
A calculated hunch has finally paid off; a bullet now ripped down the line
Time to take credit where credit is due, a team player, just one of the nine.

An aerial dive, stretched out, facing grass, my body in flight, air-borne
Talent has always come natural to me, like magic, damn, what a throw!
I constantly struggle to try and be humble, unequalled, unrivalled, no match
Great call at first by the big man in blue, thrown out by a step, nice stretch.

The "Franchise" approaches the batter's box, no sweat, there's now two away
With a one-run lead, the game's in the bag, but man this guy can play.
He lives for this moment, digs in at the plate; his smile spells full out attack
He points his Louisville out to the mound and wisely I take a step back.

My perfect smile has since disappeared; no doubt, the ball is destined for me
It's just an ugly feeling you get, when you reside down at sack number three.
His spikes come alive, he's carving up dirt, it's a game within a game right now
Coiled and poised, he's ready to strike; cool sweat trickles down through my brow.

The first ball thrown is close, but inside, oh yeah, let's put this guy on
The last pitch looked pretty good to me; chances are the next one is gone.
Scouting reports say low and outside, he'll chase it, let's stay in the park
Just steer the ball clear of this brave third baseman, now taking stock of his heart.

Pride of course, forms the back of the line, as I adjust my crotch and spit
My agent collared big dollars for me, as I finally learned how to hit.
But chills feel eerie on a hot summer day; the game is at last understood
My alleged, legendary, defensive skills had best be equally good.

Clarity came with a wake-up call; the game can't be summed up in stats
His answer came with the piercing sound of an unmistakable bat.
The ball screamed towards me at lightning speed, a laser of blinding light
My choice was clear, retire the side, or be monitored each hour, overnight.

The fans suspect I'm for real, and why not? Some stare in sheer disbelief
It's far from another day at the park, when a ball whistles in at your teeth.
But again I'm there to make a great catch; did anyone have any doubt?
My memoirs are surely to follow, but for now I'll just play the game out!

~ RWM

CHAPTER 14

~

BASEBALL AND ME

My hopes and dreams for a Major League career were downsized somewhat to a lower profile version of baseball stardom. After twelve years of playing the game at various age levels (8-10 in the minors [as they called it back then], 10-12 in Little League, 13-15 in Babe Ruth, and finally Connie Mack, where the 16-18 year olds turned prematurely gray), I had no choice but to retire. A number of others who found themselves in the very same position as me followed my example. With nowhere else to turn, we played the only game available to us at that time which was fastball.

Curiously, the scouts had stayed away in droves, and the Yankees, I've recently concluded, had somehow misplaced my name in their secret directory of aspiring baseball phenoms. Hardball had been the only game in town for me and all the guys I grew up with. But fastball or softball was to me, a surprisingly new, highly competitive version of the game I still loved. Even more surprising, it turned out to be an unexpected but welcome challenge. For many of us it extended our faded careers for another ten to fifteen years. The time frame in which the games were played made it not only a pleasant but abrupt change for us but for our legion of fans as well. I made the switch to fastball in the early Seventies and continued to play the game with a keen interest for the next eleven years.

As I mentioned, the ballplayers from the organized hardball leagues we had played in as kids were left with nowhere to play once we reached the age of nineteen. This situation, as many will remember (and even more who won't) came on the heels of the Sixties, an era emblazoned with free spirits, countless freaks and eccentric characters champing at the bit to play ball again. To say this was a smoke-free zone would be a complete misrepresentation of the facts. Whatever inspired the ex-jocks and one-time hippies of the greater Vancouver area to come together with baseball as their common denominator is beyond me, but it happened!

This miraculous collaboration resulted in an extraordinary new baseball league that appropriately called itself, the Cosmic League. The co-ordination it took to arrange games, times and parks throughout the Lower Mainland when you take into consideration the coordinators themselves, still baffles the mind. So many times we showed up eager and ready to play and found not only the other team mysteriously absent but a ballpark that had somehow vanished into thin air. Too many times the scramble was on to find a pay phone and determine very quickly, what the hell was going on. Sorry, no texting, no cellphones, or any type of social media back then. Fortunately, in many instances, we would find a payphone and contact a brother, mother or girlfriend who vaguely remembered something about a baseball game. We would check our coordinates and with hazy directions, eventually locate the right park. What we found more often than not was six or seven long-haired, bearded players huddled together waiting to play ball. It appeared more often than not that they were sending smoke signals to the heavens. Hang-dog red eyes that would be welcomed in any Clear Eyes®commercial, now eager to get going. Where the hell had we been and "hey man, can we borrow some bats?"

On more than one occasion we would find ourselves lending them a player or two with a simple reminder that nine players were still required for the current version of the game. In this world anyway! So many of them appeared to belong to another. But I have to say, I wasn't surprised that there were so many good players in the area left with no alternatives. Our roster carried quite a few. As a result, the caliber of baseball, although it varied from team to team, was played at a reasonably high level. No one would have guessed, having caught wind of the untraditional names taken by the teams, that the competition would be intensely fierce. Win at all costs!

We all had the same motto but differing views of the currency. Umpires were most often drafted from the bleachers, or a player, unless he was busy lighting up, took a turn handling the bases or behind home plate. Of course the arguments were ongoing and at times, heated but the scuffles were kept to a minimum. I can remember only one fist fight.

Regretfully, or perhaps by choice, I won't repeat the name of our own team here in print. That alone should give you a fair indication. Don't get me wrong, we were proud of the name. We took a team vote and it was unanimous. We loved it and so did most of our fans. Thirty years later a few of us still have our original T-shirts with the H.O.'s proudly displayed on the front and our winged logo emblazoned on the back. They hardly fit anymore but have come to be collectors' items nonetheless. Prized possessions and family heirlooms at least in our circle anyway.

Some years ago the local RCMP approached us during a game while we were participating in a tournament in Pemberton, B.C., and asked us if we would kindly remove our shirts. They had received complaints and apparently some people were offended. We reluctantly agreed but would comply only after our current game had been completed. It seems the focal point of the complaints centered on the logo, which as I mentioned, was displayed on the back of our jerseys. Apparently the letters spelling it out in full on the front of our jerseys was acceptable. In hindsight, perhaps the name on the front didn't help us garner many new fans after all. We won that game but after removing our identity, we lost the next game. It was time to man up! We put them back on for the next contest and never heard another word about it. It worked and we won our next game as well and figured the power had been restored. We were eliminated shortly after. We were slated to play the last game of the day but the officials approached us and informed us that the game being played at the moment was going into extra innings and the next game would soak up all of the remaining daylight. Our game was moved to the following morning. After all there were no lights, so night games were obviously non-existent. This was great news as there was a dance that evening and we now had more time to prepare.

Most teams were camped out in the open grass beyond the one playing field Pemberton had at that time. We had more than knocked back a few beverages before the very same officials were seen approaching us once again. The extra inning game had somehow come to a quick ending and after that, what was supposed to have been be the final game of the day was stopped early on account of the seven run rule. That's right, sports fans! Our postponed game was not only back on, but would be starting within the half hour. I can still remember our shortstop trying to stand at his position without falling over backwards. At least I think that was him. There seemed to be two of everything. Anyway, we lost but returned to the Pemberton tournament for many years after that.

There was an Indian presence in Pemberton as it was home to a reservation nearby on the Mount Currie Reserve. They always had a team entered in the annual competition and damned if they didn't fit right in name wise as they called themselves the Wagon Burners. They were always tough to beat and extremely quick on the bases. Members of The Mount Currie Band not on the baseball team always and without fail volunteered to umpire the games. These fellas really knew their baseball and were undoubtedly some of the best umpires we had ever encountered anywhere in our travels. As most baseball fans will recognize, that is a statement not made lightly.

Randy McLean of College Place, seen here receiving an all-star trophy at recent Port Coquitlam Mueen's fastball tournament, will be in the line-up for College Place when they take part in the sixteen team senior men's fastball tournament at Telosky Stadium in Haney Friday, Saturday, and Sunday.

All-Star Second Base Trophy in one hand, beer in the other.

As for the Cosmic League, fortunately, a few names of the teams in our humble League were acceptable for print. A much too-short list of the least offensive names included Flex Morgan, the Queensborough Queens, the Rapid City Ramblers, Patterson Avenue Perverts and the Bum Biters. Despite the dizzying array of names, the teams were exceptionally talented and serious when they took the field. Although our name wasn't suitable for print, our record certainly was. We had a lifetime of fun but between the lines we were all business.

After eleven memorable (an understatement) and extremely fulfilling Cosmic years, I returned to Blue Mountain Park in Coquitlam, B.C. This was my old stomping grounds and I coached Babe Ruth baseball for three satisfying years at some of the old parks I had played in as a kid. At the time, I didn't really feel I was giving anything back to the sport, although in some small way, I suppose I was. I enjoyed it so much. Not everyone that signs up to play organized baseball is destined to be a star. The odds are definitely stacked against you. So, in my few years as a coach, I tried to make sure the kids had fun and enjoyed what they were learning on the field. When they least expected it, I would slip in some of the finer points of the game hoping to further their finite careers.

It always helped that Joe, my buddy and fellow coach, was not only a great organizer but my saving grace. He made me look good each and every day. We played a watered-down version of good cop, bad cop. We discussed every move to the last detail but thankfully, he volunteered to handle the parents and any discipline that might be needed. He had a lovely wife, two great kids, a house and a dog, and I'm convinced he was better prepared for the task than I was. No kidding! I was thrilled and flattered he asked me to assist him in coaching as he knew my resume held quite a few years of playing the game at various levels. However, I was still single and loving it. I guess my ultimate goal was to try and make sure that after the kids' playing days were over, they would not only pass on the redeeming qualities of the game to close friends and relatives, but someday instill the passion and beauty of the game into their own kids. I wanted them to be able to look back with a sense of satisfaction and pride. I wanted the kids to eventually realize that they had taken part in and would continue to follow a game that welcomes all of us with open arms at any level for a lifetime and then some. At least until that unfortunate moment when we are all quietly laid to rest. Even then, for all we know, the moments may continue and the hits might keep on coming. Baseball Heaven!

If the true measure of our coaching influence was indeed successful, their final will and testament might insist that they be buried with their musty, worn-out glove, a Louisville Slugger or a perhaps a tattered piece of paper with a favorite autograph eternally sprawled out on their chest. Well, so much for privacy and the final contents of my own will. In a final summation of the game, baseball great and author Jim Bouton of "Ball Four" fame, once summed up his heartfelt passion for the game he loved in this way: "You see, you spend a good piece of your life gripping a baseball, and in the end it turns out that it was the other way around all the time." One of my favorite quotes!

~

143

WARMING UP TO HISTORY

The important player on every team, is always the shortstop or pitcher
Ask him today where he plays he'll say, the position I'm in, getting richer.
So much has changed; it's different these days, expensive new contracts for one
Tell me, what can I take from this game? Seems to be the mantra for some.

The games have become so impersonal; the history of the sport seems lost
It can't be the spikes and gloves they prefer, nor the bats and balls they toss.
Three-piece Armani's and flashy "smart" toys hold minor assets for the team
Respect and heart is a rare place to start; let's see how good you can be!

Great players past in days long gone, survived with a second income
The game has evolved, they play a short time, retire with money and then some.
A few hone their skills and master their craft; I won't paint the League with one brush
But man, you're alive in a fantasy camp, go hit a home run in the clutch!

I'd sell off my soul, why, wouldn't you? While most take their stature for granted
My Kingdom for talent, now that's a fair trade, a bargain not got from "Dear Santa."
So think about this, it's your moment in time; step up before it's too late
Yes this is Heaven, it's not Iowa, it's your dream, now go out and play!

Chance comes but once, blink, and it's gone; wake up, you're missing your call
Down through the ages they both have stood tall, the magic of life and baseball.
Opportunity knocks, the window's wide open, the game's not a big mystery
It's time to come clean; it's never too late, warm up to the game's history.

~ RWM

CHAPTER 15

~

REMEMBERING

When I touched down at La Guardia airport Saturday, September 8, 2001, my itinerary for the first few days called for me to be staying in the Woodside area of Queens. Early Tuesday morning, September 11, 2001, I was all set to embark upon another journey. An adventurous bus ride to the Baseball Hall of Fame in Cooperstown, some five hours away in upstate New York. A virtual Disneyland for baseball fans. I had no time to turn the TV on that morning, so upon checkout, I was shaken to see the North Tower of the World Trade Center in smoke on the television behind the hotel counter. Shortly after, the second plane hit the South Tower and I knew I wouldn't be going anywhere that day. It wasn't a tough decision to check back in and I sat alone in shock for the remainder of the day.

At one point during the early afternoon, I chanced a look out of my hotel room window and was surprised to see crowds of people in obvious despair walking along Queens Boulevard. Woodside Station in Queens is one of the above-ground terminals for the 7 Train and as all the underground stations were prohibited for travel due to the possibility of furthers threats that day, Woodside became a dropping-off point for a countless number of people looking to leave Manhattan. Many people found themselves walking great distances to get home to loved ones that day. Many were in search of somewhere to stay. Checking back in was a good decision for me but as I found out later, many more were unfortunately turned away. There were no rooms left for those guilty only of seeking safe shelter. For hours on end I was glued to the television set. Eyes raw from wiping tears away but thankful that I was one of the lucky ones. I had been to the top of the World Trade Center on a previous visit and had been within a few blocks just two days earlier. Now it was gone.

I ventured out sometime in the afternoon as I realized I had yet to eat. I sat down to attempt a late breakfast but before the waitress even got to me I was overcome. Tears came for whatever and all reasons and I was unable to stop for some minutes. I knew I wasn't the only one. The waitress gave me some time and when she approached me, she asked if I was alright. Did I know someone in the Trade Center? I didn't, but I just wasn't gathering it all in at that point. For me, that alone had been enough to start the waterworks. She was kind for asking and incredibly understanding. The breakfast was a memorable one for more reasons than hunger alone.

Later that evening, I just had to get out and get some air. I found myself stepping into the local Irish pub (I wish I could remember the name) and found I wasn't the only one who just had to seek out human contact. It was a somewhat somber mood but people just had to talk to someone. Anyone! They had to at least try and set things straight in their own heads, or make sense of something so far beyond comprehension. Was this really happening? Unfortunately, the news broadcasts and the world outside helped us all find the answer to that question. Sometime later (the hours were getting fuzzy), I was able to contact the Lakefront Motel on Lake Otsego in Cooperstown to inform them that I would not be able to make it this year. It would be an understatement to say they were more than understanding of the situation. The owner not only waived my reservation with short notice, but upon my arrival back in Vancouver, I found they had fully refunded the deposit I had sent a month earlier. I promised myself that I would definitely be back.

I had been in New York City for two weeks and as my departure date neared, I approached the idea of flying with more than a little apprehension. I mentioned this to a friend of mine back in Vancouver and asked him if hopping a train might not only be a wiser but more importantly, a safer mode of transportation for getting back home. It had been a few days since 9/11 and he told me that flying, in fact, might be the most secure way of traveling at this point. Flights had been taking off and landing now at La Guardia for a few days, but to say things were back to normal was stretching the truth somewhat. His answer was well thought out and made complete sense to me considering the trumped-up security that was being employed at every airport in the U.S., Canada, and throughout the world. So I took his advice along with a cab to the airport and proceeded to check in.

The airport had a tense, formal, but dignified feel in the air as I awaited my turn for check in. The lineups were moving slowly as expected. Caution was at a peak and all means of identification were checked and rechecked. People still went about their business in a professional manner but it didn't feel the same. There was a definite police presence on this day with security at the highest level. A presence that survives to this day as passenger safety is front and center in our changing world. The NYPD was everywhere with most of them fully armed. People took more notice of their surroundings but no more than yours truly. In my eyes, everyone looked like they were up to no good. The announcements seemed to ring out every half hour or so, reminding people that if they saw anything peculiar or anyone suspicious, to report it immediately. As far as I was concerned, everyone looked suspicious. I saw hundreds of people in the airport that day that I hoped weren't on the same flight as me. As it turned out, it seemed like they were all on my flight.

I will never forget the sight of the toughest-looking New York City policeman, sporting the meanest-looking brush cut I have ever seen cruising about the departure area. He was an obvious standout in the airport crowd. Harsh in appearance with intimidation written all over him. He would have stood out in a crowd of Hell's Angels but the Kevlar vest, German shepherd held tight on a leash and shotgun resting on his hip pointing skyward made him the poster boy for "don't f— with New York!" You would have been a fool to step out of line or look at him sideways but for some reason, he felt like my best friend that morning.

We had a planned stopover in Minneapolis to change planes for the last leg of our trip to Vancouver. I really didn't want to stop as obviously the plane we were on was staying airborne to everyone's complete satisfaction. What was supposed to have been a short layover was starting to drag on when the announcement came that they were having some problems with the plane we were to board. However, they would start boarding shortly.

Sometime later, they announced that this particular plane was now being replaced. They were bringing another plane out of the hanger and again, we would be boarding very soon. I had heard that somewhere before. The next announcement was to inform us that the plane they had brought out was no longer an option. They didn't explain why but it didn't really matter. Imaginations were running wild by that time. Finally, the announcement came that very shortly, a flight would be arriving at Minneapolis-St. Paul International Airport direct from San Jose, and that plane would fly us safely to Vancouver International. I was quite relieved as I figured that if this plane landed safely in Minnesota, then at least there was proof it could fly. It was a long trip home to Vancouver but a very acceptable final result. I have never been so happy to feel rubber touching the runway. Home at last!

~

2001 was a year most of us will never forget and that is how it should be. We all know where we were the moment we became aware of the events unfolding and it will stay with us. As time struggles forward, it is and always will be a part of who we are regardless of our background or what country you may find yourself in. I found myself in New York City visiting for the fourth time just three days before 9/11. To say it was a terrible time for the city seems like such an understatement, and it is. But what words can we conjure up that truly encapsulate the tragedy that struck that day. Some brilliant writers have somehow found the words and put them to print. I have read quite a few of them. They still bring tears to my eyes. They have a gift for expression under difficult circumstances, but I am not one of them.

I tried hard to endure the wave of emotions just like everyone else that bore witness to that day and the troubled days that followed. The highs and lows of all emotions were laid bare on the streets, in the stores, subways, sidewalks and restaurants and any face you encountered for countless days and nights. At times I felt like an intruder to such a personal tragedy for so many. I would soon come to realize the heart and soul of New York City. I will never forget the heartbreak on the faces of friends and family, holding up photographs of loved ones, wandering the streets, desperate for news. Holding onto the faint hope that maybe, just maybe, their future may still hold some promise of light. Unfortunately, very few were rewarded.

I will never forget the pictures posted outside of the cities' many fire halls. Proud, sometimes smiling faces of firemen recently lost just a few precious hours before, at what was now Ground Zero. They were proudly displayed on the walls outside of many local fire stations in Queens, where I was staying as well as Manhattan and the surrounding boroughs. These brave men and women responded without question. But mostly I remember the resiliency of the people. I was proud of those who refused to give in and stood tall under trying circumstances. It couldn't have been easy and I'm sure it still isn't. My hat's off and my heart still goes out to those affected. To Rudolph Giuliani, David Letterman and many more unsung heroes for helping the City get back on its feet. There are many who still suffer and for most it will never go away. In my own small way, I came to realize that what I now humbly call my second home would never bow to the likes responsible for such madness. The sight of fighter planes flying over Manhattan is something I won't soon forget. It was comforting in an odd way to feel their presence but the reason for them being there sucked. I have never forgotten nor regretted any day spent in New York City or State. The residents of New York City are golden in the eyes of this Canadian boy. I will always remember.

A Manhattan street artist drew this portrait of me for $5.00

~

CHAPTER 16

~

DOUBLE X

In a few short words, my first trip to the Hall of Fame in Cooperstown, New York was in every sense of the word – fascinating! It was a lifelong dream come true for me. Upon my arrival back home in Vancouver, I realized that one name stood tall above the numerous and notable legends I had encountered. Jimmie Foxx! Oh sure, there was the Babe, Gehrig, Ty Cobb, Aaron, Mantle and Mays, and the list goes on, but Jimmie Foxx grabbed my curiosity like no other. I wasn't prepared for this. Brooks Robinson, Joe DiMaggio, Hank Greenberg of course, but who was Jimmie Foxx? I'd heard the name many times throughout the years, but what astounded me was the relative obscurity his memory resided in, when immortality was right at his doorstep. Babe Ruth had set the baseball world on fire in the 1927 season with his record-setting 60 home runs. Five years later, Foxx had a stranglehold on his own pathway to eternal stardom as he became a very real threat to break Ruth's record. A record that would ultimately last 34 years until Roger Maris hit 61 round-trippers in 1961. To further accent this milestone's place in the record books: no one would break Maris' home run record for another 37 years until Mark McGwire and Sammy Sosa both demolished it in 1998. (In an era where steroid use is still being uncovered, McGwire and Sosa's achievements, including Barry Bonds further record-breaking numbers, have become more than dubious and in many eyes and their place in the record books is extremely questionable).

I can only dream of bringing to life on these few sheets of paper the achievements Foxx accomplished and those he pursued, but I will make the attempt. Like Foxx, we all come out on the short end of perfect, but it's the effort that truly matters, and not always the result. Besides, getting there is half the fun. Hopefully by the end of this article, even if I've revealed only a glimpse or a shimmer of the bright light this man represented, I will have succeeded. Jimmie Foxx's career was brilliant and distinguished, but his personal life was not always that way. I'm sure Foxx would have you shed no tears, for he took the world with all its gifts and foibles and accepted them without question. He was a gentle, bighearted, giant of a man who treated everyone as an equal and expected no special exemptions because of who he was or what he was able to deliver on the baseball field. Both feet were planted firmly on the ground and he was literally loved by all who knew him. The reverence bestowed upon him by his friends and peers was a testament to that fact. The man who was affectionately called the "Beast" or "Double X" was not only a sensation on the field of play, but a very real player in the game of life.

It's no coincidence that Babe Ruth and Roger Maris set their records in Yankee Stadium, a park that has maintained a shallow fence in right field throughout its historic existence. This is in no way an attempt to take anything away from these two men, as their home run records stand tall and were well deserved. Ruth played in eight fewer games than Roger, but Maris was playing under constant threats from baseball fans (New Yorkers included). If the record was broken, the fans apparently would have preferred someone they considered more worthy, should the Babe be relieved of his historic mark. This was undue pressure no athlete would prefer to endure. Both men, especially Ruth, could hit mammoth shots, and their home runs in all likelihood surely would have cleared the fences in any baseball park.

This brings us back to Jimmie Foxx and 1932. Lawrence S. Ritter's exceptional book on old stadiums called "Lost Ballparks: A Celebration of Baseball's Legendary Fields," shows that a high number of left-field fences were clearly much deeper than the right-field fences, making it much tougher for a right hander to hit home runs than a lefty. As we all know, Ruth and Maris were left-handed batters, but there's more to Jimmie Foxx's story that many historians understandably overlook. By 1932, many American League stadiums had begun to add screens atop their outfield fences. These screens became insurmountable obstacles for Foxx in his pursuit of the infamous 60 home runs in a single season. The most notable of these parks were Briggs Stadium in Detroit, League Park in Cleveland and Sportsman's Park in St. Louis. Home runs in these parks were cut down considerably as a result. These were screens that the Babe did not have to contend with in 1927! It's been noted that Foxx lost anywhere from five to twelve home runs that were driven into these new additions. Some say he lost five homers into the screens in St. Louis alone. To further pinpoint the uncontrollable conditions which prevented Foxx from a legacy perhaps not meant to be, was the fact that two home runs which he had already hit in a game, were erased due to a rain out in Detroit. It was called before a complete game could be recorded. These two homers alone would have equaled Ruth's amazing record. These unfortunate setbacks were events that, not surprisingly to those who knew him, left Foxx totally unfazed. Opponents and teammates agree that Jimmie Foxx was nothing if not good natured on and off the field and extremely well-liked by those around him. Sportswriter Al Hirschberg once wrote, "His personality was one of the gentlest in the game. Foxx hated no one and no one hated him. From the day he first went into the Major Leagues, he was pleasant to everyone, never impatient with fans or admirers, and always, always accessible to anybody who appreciated him."

It would be an obvious understatement to say there was only one Babe Ruth. There never was, and never will be another to compare with him. That is a fact! He was larger than life, and made himself accessible to fans and sportswriters alike, giving his time to everyone with personality to spare and a boatload of charm. The Babe simply loved being the Babe. Jimmie Foxx was never bitter about coming up short of the record and in fact, never begrudged any man his accomplishments. Especially Ruth. The Babe is likely the most recognized name in all of sport and always will be. There were candy bars, children and baseball youth leagues named after him, and rightly so.

Jimmie Foxx never thought of himself as an equal to the Babe, in fact he always maintained he never really tried to hit home runs. As a point of interest, he actually put Ruth on a pedestal far above himself. In Foxx's own words, "...but if I had broken Ruth's record, it wouldn't have made any difference. Oh, it might have put a few more dollars in my pocket, but there was only one Ruth."

But let's not forget about one of the mightiest right-handed batters of all time. A man who became just the second player in history to reach 500 home runs, before finally ending his career with 534. Hall of Fame catcher and former New York Yankee Bill Dickey once said of Foxx, "If I were catching blindfolded, I'd always know when it was Foxx who connected. He hit the ball harder than anyone else."

In the decade of the 1930s alone, "Double X" hit a staggering 415 home runs, and accumulated 1,403 of his 1,922 career total RBI. During the year of his home run chase in 1932, his slugging percentage was an unheard of .749. An amazing feat! He was one of only four Major Leaguers who had reached the .700 mark for slugging in three separate seasons. Although he was often called the right-handed Babe Ruth, he was more comfortable with "Double X" than the "Beast". The latter being a testament to his strength, and certainly not his demeanor.

Jimmie Foxx's entry into the Hall of Fame, along with fellow inductee Mel Ott in 1951, was an obvious choice and a definite acknowledgment of his achievements on the field, but somehow that just doesn't speak loudly enough for a legend of his magnitude. This man's name should ring over hill and dale and echo throughout the fields of every baseball park ever built, past or present. This is his story.

James Emory Foxx was born on October 22, 1907, in the small farming community of Sudlersville, Maryland. As a kid growing up he was said to have jump-started his legendary strong man status by toiling away on his father's farm. At the tender age of 10, with WWI raging in Europe, the spirited Foxx tried to enlist in the army. After naturally being turned down, he then turned his attention to sports; track and field in particular. It was there that he developed the powerful legs which would not only help in propelling his home runs into countless bleachers in the years to come, but turn him into one of the quickest base runners in the game.

Baseball had always been extremely good to Jimmie, and by the time he was 17 years old he was playing high school ball for Easton (Maryland) of the Eastern Shore League. The manager of that team happened to be none other than recently retired and Future Hall of Fame third baseman, Frank "Home Run" Baker. Baker had enjoyed a fine and productive career with the Philadelphia A's and New York Yankees, and while toiling in Philly he played under a man named Cornelius McGillicudy, or as he was more widely known, Connie Mack. Mack, himself a future Hall of Famer, and Baker were close friends with a mutual respect for each other's knowledge of the game, and it was Baker who recommended Foxx to the baseball savvy Mack. Mr. Mack had an uncanny eye for talent and wasn't about to let Foxx get away. He signed the powerful right-hander and brought him up to Philadelphia for a 10-game stint as an 18-year-old catcher in 1925. Foxx hit .667, but while he didn't stick right away, was brought up for games in 1926 and 1927 before permanently joining the club for the start of the 1928 season. The rest, as they say, is history. At the time, Mack was caught up in his own dilemma as he already had one of the best catchers in the game by the name of Mickey Cochrane. Cochrane was a team leader, a fierce competitor and a future Hall of Famer as well. Connie Mack had no alternatives and eventually advised the new young catcher to get himself a first baseman's mitt. The catcher's job was spoken for. Although Foxx caught over 100 games during his career in the Major Leagues, he would spend most of his time at first and third base. Jimmie took the move with nonchalance and a quiet grace. He just wanted to play, and most always did what he was told. In Connie Mack's own words, "He is the easiest boy on the team to handle... does whatever I ask...plays any position and never complains."

It was no coincidence that further successes were just around the corner for the Philadelphia A's, with a lineup that included Foxx and Cochrane, as well as slugger Al Simmons, pitchers George Earnshaw, Rube Walberg and the great Lefty Grove. Foxx and the A's did in fact, win the American League pennant in 1929, 1930 and 1931 while simultaneously capturing World Series titles in the '29 and '30 seasons. Although Foxx was mostly proud of his World Series victories, individual awards did find their way into his illustrious resume. He won the American League MVP award in Philly during the 1932 (58 HR, 169 RBI, .364 Avg.), and 1933 (48HR, 163 RBI, .356 Avg.) seasons, and once again in 1938, (50 HR, 175 RBI, .349 Avg.) two years after being traded to the Boston Red Sox. He also topped the .700 mark in slugging for each of those coveted MVP seasons.

Since 1901, a mere twelve players have won the prestigious Triple Crown award, the ultimate accolade in hitting prowess, with only Rogers Hornsby and Ted Williams winning it twice. Miguel Cabrera became the most recent member of the club in 2012, the first player to win the award since Carl Yastrzemski did it in 1967. Jimmie Foxx won the award during his MVP season in 1933, but except for an unfortunate string of events, the Sudlersville slugger would have garnered two more Triple Crowns. For inexplicable reasons, the 1932 batting title was awarded to Dale Alexander with his .367 batting average, beating out Foxx by a slim three percentage points. What makes it so strange is the fact that Alexander, who had only 16 at bats with Detroit before being traded to Boston, where he accumulated an additional 376 at bats, never reached the 400 official at bats, or the 502 plate appearances needed to qualify for the title. Foxx was robbed of what would have been his first Triple Crown award as he had the home run and RBI titles cinched. Jimmie Foxx never complained or questioned the result. While with Boston during his 1938 MVP season, he had the batting title and RBI title once again, but lost what would have been his third Triple Crown when the Detroit Tigers' Hank Greenberg mounted his own assault on the Babe's 60 home run season. Greenberg was stopped short with a still impressive 58 dingers. Foxx came up shy of the home run title with 50. Greenberg's 58 in 1938 did tie Jimmie's record for home runs for a right-handed batter set in 1932. (This was a record they shared until 1998, when Sosa and McGwire passed the mark.)

Like most sluggers, "Double X" led the American League in strikeouts seven different times, as many of the power hitters before and after him were inclined to do. But the 1,311 strikeouts and the 1,452 walk totals make his 534 home runs and 2,646 hits in 8,134 at bats even more incredible. When he connected, the results were staggering. His 1,751 runs scored, and .428 on base percentage serves notice to not only his speed, but his keen eye at the plate. He was no slouch when he took to the field either, as his .990 lifetime fielding percentage, while playing three different positions, will attest to. He drove in 100 or more runs thirteen times and topped the 30 HR and 100 RBI marks in twelve consecutive seasons. Consecutive! He was elected to the All-Star game every year from 1933-1941, batted .344 in his three World Series appearances and held the mark for the youngest player in history to reach 500 HR at 32 years, 11 months and 2 days for many years. (New York Yankee third baseman Alex Rodriguez, another right-handed batter, has since broken this record at 32 years and 8 days.)

Jimmie Foxx hit his very first home run on May 31, 1927, off of New York Yankees right-handed pitcher Urban Shocker in the second game of a double-header. Foxx's Philadelphia A's lost both of those games to the Yanks as a gentleman named Babe Ruth connected for homers in both contests. Jimmie went on to hit monster shots everywhere he played and it seemed every American League park had a Jimmie Foxx story to tell. As Lefty Gomez once proclaimed, "I was pitching one day when my glasses clouded up on me. I took them off to polish them. When I looked up to the plate, I saw Jimmie Foxx. The sight of him terrified me so much that I haven't been able to wear glasses since." Gomez fell victim to the Double X trademark and witnessed countless other home runs. Foxx once hit a ball off of Gomez, in Yankee Stadium that reached far into the upper deck and actually broke a seat in the next to last row, just left of the bullpen area. He was said to have hit one of the longest balls ever hit in Detroit, and in Chicago's Comiskey Park, he hit a ball over the double-decked bleachers that eventually cleared 34th Street outside the stadium walls.

Babe Ruth's legendary mystique was further enhanced by his often questioned "called shot" against the Chicago Cubs on October 1, 1932. It was in the fifth inning of the third game of the World Series, when he was said to have pointed to the outfield fence and subsequently hit the next pitch off of Cubs pitcher Charlie Root over that very same wall. All the while enduring constant heckling from the Cub players. Similarly, the "Beast" himself turned teddy bear when, prior to the 1929 World Series, during a press interview, he announced his own edition of a "called shot" when he predicted a home run for his newborn child, Jimmie Jr. He kept that promise when he homered off of, oddly enough, the same Charlie Root, for the A's first run in the first game of the Series. Philadelphia eventually won that Fall Classic over the Cubs in five games.

"Double X" stood deep in the batters' box with a wide stance and a full stride into the ball. His arms were visibly flexed as the ball made its way to the plate and he made sure his sleeves were cut short in apparent intimidation. Yankee teammates, Bill Dickey and Lefty Grove once huddled with a waiting Jimmie Foxx standing patiently at the plate. As catcher Dickey approached the pitcher's mound he asked Grove, "Well, what do you want to throw him?" Grove's response was, "I don't want to throw him nothin'. Maybe he'll just get tired of waitin' and leave!"

During the 1934 All-Star game, screwball pitcher Carl Hubbell gained legendary status by striking out Babe Ruth, Lou Gehrig, Jimmie Foxx, Al Simmons and Joe Cronin (all future Hall of Famers) in brief succession. It was Foxx, however, who claimed the only bragging rights amongst the sluggers. He was the only one to hit a foul ball!

On April 14, 1933, Foxx hit for the cycle driving in 9 runs to break, at that time, the record of 8, set by Roy Hartzell on July 12, 1911. (A record-setting 8 men hit for the cycle in 1933.) During Foxx's tenure with the A's, and despite their success, there was no big money to be made in Philadelphia, as the team was somehow, financially strapped. Before the start of the 1936 season, Connie Mack traded "Double X" to Tom Yawkey's Boston Red Sox where he was finally well paid for his exceptional skills. It was during his time in Boston that he took a young lad by the name of Ted Williams under his wing. The easygoing Foxx and the brash rookie had an obvious personality difference, but even the self-serving Williams had to admit, "I truly loved Foxxie."

Unfortunately, although Jimmie Foxx was never a rich man, he drank heavily and never failed to pick up the tab. He did fail in his many business ventures and what little money he did have, always seemed to disappear. As teammate and Boston second baseman Bobby Doerr once exclaimed, "Jimmie was a big spender! He would always be the one to pick up the tab whenever we went out for steaks at Durgin Park (Boston) or wherever. It was not unusual for him to call out, 'The drinks are on the house – old 'Double X' is here!'"

After a sparkling 20-year career in Major League baseball, Jimmie Foxx played his last game on September 23, 1945. His career had taken him to Philadelphia from 1926 through to the 1935 seasons, until his trade to Boston in time for the 1936 season, where he stayed until 1942. With WWII still seemingly far from over in Europe, Foxx volunteered for the military in 1944, but again was turned down due to a nagging sinus condition that had plagued him for many years. In 1945 he returned to baseball and Philadelphia. This time playing for the National League Phillies. On August 20, 1945, near the end of his storied career, he got permission to pitch and started a game for those same Phillies. Foxx pitched his heart out for

6 and 2/3rd innings before finally beating the Cincinnati Reds 4-2. In that '45 season, he appeared in nine games as a pitcher, and in 22 2/3rd innings, finished with 10 strikeouts and an ERA of 1.59. The man could just flat out play the game!

Unfortunately, it was the end of the line for his playing career, so the natural progression was for him to try and stay involved in the game he truly loved. He turned to broadcasting for a time and when that didn't work out, became coach of the Bridgeport Connecticut Bees in the Colonial League. From there he embarked on a unique coaching career with the Fort Wayne (Indiana) Daisies of the All-American Girls Professional League. His affable nature was a perfect fit for the girls and they responded to his knowledge and abilities. Although many creative freedoms were taken, it has been said that the Tom Hanks role in the major motion picture, "A League of Their Own," starring Geena Davis and Madonna, was based on Jimmie Foxx.

Foxx, along with New York Giants standout Mel Ott, was elected to the Baseball Hall of Fame in January, 1951. Although it was a deserved choice, it brought with it no immediate riches. His drinking had created problems for himself both on and off the field. Speculation is all we can muster while pondering what additional accolades could have been tagged onto an already sensational career had it not been for alcohol, and the aggravating sinus condition that continually haunted him. It's entirely possible that either one of those problems may have been responsible for the other. Jimmie Foxx remained a true gentleman and never looked for sympathy from anyone. Despite his many problems, he never changed his gentle outlook or his quiet demeanor.

In 1958, Jimmie Foxx found himself completely out of work and unable to pay his rent. The Boston chapter of the Baseball Writers Association revealed this heart-breaking news and within hours, job offers poured in from all over the country. It was at this time, Foxx himself reflected on his many years in baseball and where he stood at this present point in time. "Well, I earned $275,000 playing baseball and I don't have a dime to show for 20 years in the game. I don't feel badly for myself. The money I lost – and blew – was my own fault. 99 percent of it. Suddenly, your 50 years old and nobody wants you. So athletes have to put something away. You only stay up there so long. It's always nice to have the crowds on your side, but it doesn't last long once you stop producing."

Shortly after hearing the news, his old friends Tom Yawkey and Joe Cronin of the Boston Red Sox called, offering him a coaching job with the Minneapolis Millers, a Boston farm club. Foxx never did make a lot of money throughout his Major League career, but refused to complain or become bitter. In his own words, "Baseball was mighty good to me but I was born 10 years too soon."

Not long after Willie Mays had surpassed his home run total of 534, (at that time only the third player to reach the 500 plateau) Foxx endorsed the future Hall of Famer. "I hope Mays hits 600. For 25 years they thought only left-handers could hit the long ones. They even teach right-handed young-sters to hit left." He may have been prophetic as Mays ended his career with 660 home runs.

Sadly, it seems that the great Jimmie Foxx has been unduly overlooked and sometimes forgotten until one of his many personal achievements or historic records is passed or broken. At moments like that it appears the history of the game and a great many of its heroes are lost forever. A man of his stature, and Hall of Fame ballplayer of his caliber, should never, ever be forgotten. The game prides itself, and is entirely built on its history and can only sustain itself if its past heroes and stars are remembered. Records speak for themselves, but except for a few unfortunate events, Jimmie Foxx would be spoken of in the same breath as the Babe. One thing is for certain, he was never underestimated or underappreciated by his teammates, his opponents, or the extremely fortunate fans that were privileged enough to have watched him play.

James Emory Foxx died on July 21, 1967, while dining with his brother in Miami, Florida. He reportedly choked on a piece of meat and passed away while en route to Baptist Hospital. He was 59 years of age. What Babe Ruth and Jimmie Foxx had in common was the ability to generate and radiate an electricity the entire ballpark felt when either of them came to the plate. Jimmie Foxx, the man, the memory, the legend and the very air he breathed, will be sorely missed.

It wasn't so much the man in the uniform, the icon, the life, the good fortune or the bad luck. He took life as it came, and faced it head on! That, for me, made for one of the most genuine human beings I have ever come across. This man was a baseball Hall of Famer if there ever was one! His heroics on the field sometimes took an uncharacteristic back seat to the man himself. Jimmie Foxx, as a ballplayer, was perfect, but like every one of us, Jimmie Foxx, the man, was far from perfect. That is what makes him such an extraordinary individual!

> *"When Neil Armstrong first set foot on the moon, he and all the space scientists were puzzled by an unidentifiable white object. I knew immediately what it was. That was a home-run ball hit off me in 1937 by Jimmie Foxx."*
>
> *-Lefty Gomez*

~

ONLY A NUMBER

At times I thought I could do it
It's unanimous, the talent was there
The cards were dealt and I played them
Few records are meant to be shared.
Immortality revealed itself
The door was thrown wide open
Good fortune appeared within reach
But dreams were meant to be broken.
The world fell in love with the Babe
A man no Foxx could replace
It was close, just not in the stars
Breaks tend to decide the case.
Sixty was clearly symbolic
Who thought I'd have to explain?
I was less than thrilled with the fences
I was helpless to thwart the rain.
Don't get me wrong, I was flattered
Greenberg was soon to find out
Down to the wire, my bat was on fire
Soon after my chances went south.
The magic I chased was clear
But I came up short, so what?
Two homers for a legacy sealed
Side by side with the Sultan of Swat.
Baseball was caught in the moment
But I didn't suit up for the fame
Let statistics fall where they may
I just went out and played the damn game!

~ RWM

CHAPTER 17

~

THE PATCH

In the early spring, all eight teams from the Royal City Fastball League had a required tournament we played in each and every year. It was a commitment we all took seriously as it helped promote the League and its teams. All our games took place in Moody Park in New Westminster, B.C., and we had a great local following. The tourney was played early in the year as most of the teams committed themselves to money tournaments in and around the Lower Mainland and throughout parts of British Columbia when the summer months eventually arrived. What made the games so attractive to so many was that a full seven inning game could be played in an hour and a half. Tournament games were regulated to an hour and twenty minutes. Fans really got their money's worth considering there was no admission charge. Concession stands, beer gardens and 50/50 draws were the main source of revenue for the League. It can be a little chilly in these parts in early May when the winds, heavy gray clouds and the inevitable rains make their appearance. Actually it can be downright cold, but the brave must adapt. Most of us never thought of using batting gloves in the batter's box back in those days but we all had them. Don't get me wrong, they were a great convenience and helped our grip considerably, but were mostly used to keep our hands from freezing while gripping an ice cold beer. Tools of the trade!

This particular weekend tried so hard to bathe us in glorious sunshine but it came in spurts and spatters with intermittent cold spells. The beer garden regardless, was once again a popular spot not only between games but even more so after games. The RCMP obviously maintains a huge presence in Canada but they also had a police presence at Moody Park. They fielded a team of local players for many years in the Royal City League. They were a great bunch of guys for the most part and sported some great individual players as well. They had some big boys and a few actually loved to have a beer after the games so they fit right in, which I'm sure was the point. We all got along great and tried hard to do so. Thinking ahead, you never knew if you might one day get pulled over. A welcome face just might wangle you some wiggle room. Although their lineup varied from week to week, they loved to get out and play. They never brought the job to the ballpark which was much appreciated as they could have filled up a paddy wagon every night if they hung around long enough. To most teams the games were the obvious priority but a beer and a puff was a popular recreation as well. A lot of great guys and some talented players made their way through the League but some unsavory characters poked their heads up once in a while.

We were approached by a good-looking kid about 23 years old after a game one night that said he had played ball back East and was looking for a team to play for out our way. He hung around and we had a few cold ones with him and his sidekick that night. He swore he was a good ballplayer and he seemed like a sturdy kid so we told him to come to practice with us on the weekend and we'd go from there. After two practices we knew we had something. Why us, we asked? He said he had seen a few games at the park and liked the way we played during and after the game. It seemed like a good fit and it was. He was a great outfielder with speed and could really hit the ball with power as well. He played all summer with us on and off the field, made friends easy and was just one of the boys. Towards the end of the season we held a dance as a fundraiser for new uniforms and tournament entry fees etc. and guess who made off with the money? Poof! Gone! Vanished, just like that! Never to be seen nor heard from ever again. A real barnstormer! Where was the RCMP when you needed them? Steve, if you're reading this, you owe the H.O.'s $500!

Anyway, we had just won our first game of the tournament over this very same RCMP team and we were feeling pretty good about ourselves. Time was bought with the win and a few of us were partaking in a few beers in the bleachers behind home plate. The next game had just started and the starting pitcher for the home team was already looking a little ragged. He was quite a character and although he had his share of drug and alcohol problems over the years, he was actually a good guy and usually a pretty effective pitcher. The distance to the mound from home plate in Major League Baseball is 60 feet 6 inches compared to fastball which is 46 feet. It might as well have been 146 feet on this day as he was nowhere near the plate with any of his pitches. The few times he did get close, the visiting team responded with the swing and ping of aluminum bats. The visitors were all over him for two runs in the first and left the bases loaded. The damage was minimal all things considered as the pitcher's defense bailed him out of what could have been game over.

We thought there was something strange about the chucker's appearance on this day and on closer examination, we detected a black patch over his right eye. How did we miss that? I guess the long hair and beard fit right in for our League so we hadn't noticed much else but zeroed in on it when the game started falling apart for him. We had noticed varying degrees in his manner of dress and demeanor before this weekend but the patch, now that was something new. He looked like a lost pirate beached on the mound, pitching for the very first time. The top of the second inning hadn't started much better for Blackbeard as he walked the first two batters on nine pitches. We were having a bit of a chuckle over all this but when he went 3-0 on the next batter, our third baseman couldn't help himself. "Hey Danny! I think you've got the patch over the wrong eye!"

All heads turned our way including Danny's and a few more chuckles ensued. He wasn't exactly having the game nor time of his life but even at that point he found humor in the game. It was all in good fun and we thought it was pretty funny except for some strange looks we got from the two ladies just two rows in front of us. Danny's mom and sister, as we found out later, didn't share in our sense of humor at that particular time. Surely they can laugh about it now.

It has been a few years since I've played competitive baseball but one of my more recent pastimes has been reading the obituary columns with a mug of black coffee nestled in front of me each morning. Sounds ghoulish but apparently I'm not the only one to do so. I guess I just want to make sure that I don't see a name that resembles and in no way sounds anything like my own on these pages. So far so good! A few months ago I noticed a familiar name and as I read further, was saddened to realize that Danny had passed on. I recognized the last name and the picture confirmed it. His face was obviously a bit older but we are all traveling down that road. Perhaps he died from natural causes. It didn't say. We've all had some moments in time or decisions we'd like to take back or maybe there are just some things we would do a little bit differently. Maybe Danny did, maybe he didn't, but I know he had many good times while he was on this side of the dirt. He had some hard years on him but as far as I know, he never missed a game or a start if he could help it. How can you not love a guy who loves baseball?

It was an odd moment reading about someone from the past and it brought back a smile and some fond memories. Strangely enough, it made me think about a joke I've heard more than once over the years about two old baseball fans. These two friends had been going to see the home team play for so long that old age had crept up on them. While traveling home one day after the game, one of them turned to the other and asked, "Do you think there is baseball in heaven?" They both thought about this and exchanged their thoughts and finally came to an agreement. Whichever of them passed on first would somehow come back and tell the other the answer to this question. Some years later the inevitable happened. One of them died and left the other to attend the games alone. That spring as the remaining baseball fan walked home alone from an afternoon game he heard a voice from overhead cry out, "Bernie! Bernie!" He stopped dead in his tracks as he recognized the voice of his old pal Walter. "Wally is that you? Have you come back to tell me the answer to our question?" "I have Bernie, but unfortunately there's some good news and some bad news." "What is it, what is it? Is there baseball in heaven?" "Well, the good news is, yes Bernie there is baseball in heaven. The bad news is you're pitching on Friday!"

Many of us do terrible things to our bodies inside and out in the name of sport or perhaps in the name of fun. Dreams of excellence, stardom, living in the moment or just a longing for endless youth can lead us down a garden path. Maybe we were naïve, suffered moments of weakness, were travelling blind or just picked the wrong friends. Maybe we were nurturing a strong case of juvenile delinquency or fooled ourselves into thinking we were just in the wrong place at the wrong time. In many instances it was just muddled dreams of immortality and callous recklessness. We all walk our own path.

It used to bother me when I'd hear parents or anyone older than me say, "...if I had it to do all over again," or "if I knew then what I know now..." but as the years pile on, I'm beginning to know exactly what they meant. If I had more energy I would walk the streets day and night looking for anyone to preach the exact same thing to. We rarely think of the end in our teens, twenties or thirties, but unfortunately, what we do will sometimes come back to haunt us. No regrets applied, because as far as I know, there are no mulligans or do-overs. You play the game, live your life, take what you get and try to make adjustments along the way. It's the nature of the beast and we all live and die with that fact. Some get lucky, others don't, but none of us gets out alive. Enjoy it while you can! As I look back, I sincerely hope that one day, maybe today, Danny's mother and sister can look back on that day and maybe, just maybe, squeeze out a tiny smile. I'm sure Danny would appreciate it and so would our third baseman.

~

BASEBALL HEAVEN

I come alive in Spring and fade again come Fall.
So much happens in between, it's tough to tell it all.
Baseball's not a game; it's a way of life for me.
Magic always happens, it's inside yourself, you see.

The sights, the sounds, the grass and the dirt.
I love it so much, the game almost hurts.
I'm a kid again, when I hear *"Play Ball!"*
It's timeless, it's life, where there's no bad calls.

The game still gives us the moments that last.
With its rich history and stars from the past.
Present day players that light up the field.
Shake hands with the future, it's one special deal.

My idols are Reggie, Cal and George Brett,
Bench, Mays and Munson, Brooks and Mike Schmidt.
Juan Marichal and the whole Oriole team.
I can't think of one of them, I wouldn't want to be.

The boys will be waiting if there is Baseball Heaven.
I've still got the arm, and I'll even bat seventh.
Friends think I'm crazy, I don't understand them,
But a good seat is a must so spread my ashes at Camden!

~ RWM

CHAPTER 18

~

THE PERFECT GIRL

In the early months of 2001, I had somehow managed to meet the absolute perfect girl for me. Is there really such a thing as the perfect girl you ask? Well, apparently so! Hard to believe at my age, but she would prove to be the love of my life. How can I explain it? Sometimes you just get lucky. When the company I worked for closed down operations after 30 years I had a choice of relocating to Alberta or retiring. I retired! At 48 years of age there was only myself to look after and it was looking like it just wasn't going to happen for me. But there she was! Like it was meant to be. The bottom line is, there's no one quite like her. I wish there were. The world would be a much a better place. I take comfort in the fact that at least my world is a much better place! My limited vocabulary chokes me up at times like this, as I find it's tough to come up with the appropriate words to describe what she means to me. If I need someone to talk to she is always there. That was important to me and a situation I was not used to finding myself in. As I've stated earlier, I found myself in New York in the days surrounding 9/11 and I really wish she had been there with me. She was a rock and somehow said all the right things at a very emotional time. Unfortunately, it was over the phone. It was at that point I realized I couldn't let her get away but the truth is, she wasn't exactly running too fast anyway. I promised myself I would try and make sure we were together from that day on. Clarity can come when you least expect it and that was my turning point.

I won't bore you with too many details, but after 57 years and counting, (there is no such thing as a confirmed bachelor) how did I get so lucky? Who knows and really, who cares? It happened and I am beyond blessed! She has a smile that won't quit and she lights up a room two steps in. After all these years, the best part of my day is seeing her face. I still run to the door when she comes home. Sweetest girl I have ever met. Her only fault is that she happens to have very poor taste in men. I guess the good news is that my taste in women is showing great promise. Her good nature and pleasant outlook allows me to pursue my dream of giving back to baseball as if it were not only my mission, but now her's as well. She has not only encouraged my obsession for baseball, but supports me in all my endeavors as I support hers. Somewhere along the way, she became an enthusiastic student of the game. To say she's an avid fan would be a huge understatement. I think she now knows more about the game than I do. I take some consolation in the fact that she had an inspired, well-informed and humble teacher. We share a passion for baseball that has held on tight and refuses to let go.

Four years ago, after ten years together, Linda and I attended a Robert Plant concert in Vancouver in April 2011. You had to be there to believe it. Plant can still belt out the songs with that timeless voice of his. He even sang a few Led Zeppelin songs for old time's sake and you'd swear Jimmy Page, John Paul Jones and John Bonham were right up there with him. Well, not quite. At that time his latest edition of musicians were called the Band of Joy and they were all of that. I had made my decision some time ago but just hours before the concert I decided to propose to Linda at a downtown restaurant and who would have guessed? She said yes! I had the waiter bring her the dessert tray and when he lifted the lid to show the ring we were both speechless. She was expecting tiramisu and I was expecting to remember the lines I had rehearsed. As I dropped (or fell) to my knees it all came back to me. Did I mention she said yes? The diners around us were surprised as well. After the applause died down and my fiancée dried her eyes we began our new life together. By ordering tiramisu!

After a few years you could hardly call it a whirlwind romance but it was a no-brainer nonetheless. The first marriage for both of us. But I had spent so much time thinking about the proposal, I hadn't entertained any talk of an actual marriage. I mean, haven't I done enough already? Most girls think about their wedding day at an early age but for me it was like driving ninety miles an hour with my hair on fire. I had no trouble with the commitment end of it but this marriage thing was beginning to sound serious. After a few short months of therapy however, I was ready to jump in with both feet. We tossed around ideas and locations for weeks. Weeks turned into months and then one night, while watching a ballgame on TV, it hit us! The announcer was talking about recent inductees and we slowly turned to each other. We knew right away what the other was thinking. It was like baseball in Iowa. It was perfect! We would soon be banded together for eternity with our decision to tie the knot within the historic confines of the Baseball Hall of Fame. It would turn out to be another dream come true! A few telephone calls and an e-mail or two later, the date was all set. I can't say enough about Cooperstown, the staff at the Baseball Hall of Fame, the Mayor and the residents of this lakeside paradise. Sales Manager June Dolhun, Director of Research Tim Wiles and the rest of the staff at the HOF treated us like long lost family. We felt so close to them that Linda asked June and I asked Tim to stand in for us during the wedding ceremony. We had no family present but our new family more than sufficed.

Joe Booan was the Mayor of Cooperstown at the time of the ceremony but as of this date, no longer holds that office. A nicer man you've never met. After first talking with him from our home in British Columbia, we knew at once that he was the man to marry us. He came to our hotel the day before the ceremony and had such a calm demeanor about him that it became entirely infectious. There was an aura of quiet confidence around him that spread throughout the HOF and ultimately brought a relaxed influence on the entire proceedings. If you met him you would immediately understand what I'm talking about. We still keep in touch and are so proud to call him a friend. After an extremely enjoyable and relaxed ceremony, Mayor Booan surprised us with a handmade baseball bat with our names, the date and "National Baseball Hall of Fame, Cooperstown, New York" inscribed forever into the wood. We now have it encased in glass and oak. It is unquestionably one of our most prized possessions. Along with the unforgettable memories! We were completely overwhelmed!

We were married September 14, 2011 within the halls of the Monument Gallery. The statues of Babe Ruth and Ted Williams presided over us and the bronze plaques and spirits of every Hall of Famer that ever graced and embraced the game of baseball were our humble ushers. The perfect day!

I turned sixty-one this year and by my count, it's now five times in which I've had the privilege of visiting the Baseball Hall of Fame and the Village of Cooperstown in upstate New York. Five times! Not bad for a poor lad from the West Coast of Canada. Every visit I discover something new. Something I inexplicably overlooked the previous times. A photograph, a baseball card, a piece of equipment, a piece of history that's as fresh today as it was the day it happened. A painting, a recording, World Series rings, statues larger than life or any of the bronze plaques gracing the walls of the Monument Gallery. It tickles me to walk through the doors and the atmosphere completely overwhelms my senses. It puts a full charge in these old batteries until I can return to Shangri-La once again. If your heart is still ticking, you can't help but be inspired. My first visit was in 1996 and I was literally in awe. Like a kid in a candy shop. I've been eating it up ever since!

~

SAY IT OUT LOUD

Cooperstown...
I saw it in a dream
Finally, safe at home.
Words can't explain
I was overwhelmed
Like a rising tide
The Baseball Hall of Fame!
Say it out loud...
Most will never feel it
What a shame.
Present meets the past...
And like that! Youth returns
I walked through history
...and so can you
But don't walk too fast.
Most will never know
But I do...
I've seen their faces
...etched in bronze.

~ RWM

REFERENCES

Baseball Rising

www.baseball-almanac.com/quotes
www.en.wikiquote.org/wiki/field_of_dreams
www.wikipedia.org

What's the Catch

www.wikipedia.org
https:/espn.go.com/sportscentury/features
www.baseball-almanac.com/quotes
www.testaae.greenwood.com/doc_print
www.yquotes.com/willie-mays
www.brainyquote.com
www.achievement.org/autodoc/page/may
www.baseball-fever.com
www.sports.espn.go.com/mlb/columns/story

A Lethal Dose (Waner Biography)

www.wikipedia.org
www.baseball-reference.com
www.baseballlibrary.com
www.baseball-almanac.com

www.thebaseballpage.com
www.easternoklahomacounty.com
www.pabooklibraries.psu.edu/palitmap/bios/waner_paul

Baker Bowl

www.thisgreatgame.com/ballparks
Baseball's Greatest Quotations by Paul Dickson
Lost Ballparks by Lawrence Ritter
www.baseball-almanac.com
www.philadelphiaathletics.org
www.baseball-fever.com
http://en.wikipedia.org
Quote by Thomas Boswell (1982)
www.research.sabr.org
Philadelphia's Old Ballparks by Rich Westcott
www.nymets.com

First Trip

www.nytimes.com
www.statisticbrain.com
www.ask.com

Opening Doors (Curt Flood Biography)

www.diamondfans.com
www2.needham.k12.ma.us/2002_p5
http://en.wikiquote.org
www.xroads.virginia.edu/~class/am483_97/projects/brady/sixties.html
www.mlquotes.com
www.quotesfriend.com
www.brainyquote.com
www.infoplease.com
www.home.earthlink.net
www.baseballlibrary.com

www.baseball-reference.com

Hank Greenberg

www.hankgreenbergfilm.org
www.wikipedia.org
www.detroitnews.com
www.baseballlibrary.com
www.lifeandtimesofh.g.-avivakempner
www.jewishaz.com
www.amuseum.org
www.baseball-almanac.com
www.baseballreference.com
www.baseballpage.cdu
www.mlb.com
www.reds.enquirer.com
www.boston.com
www.art.com
Hank Greenberg: The Story of my Life by Ira Berkow

You Never Know

www.baseball-almanac.com

Ebbett's Field

http://en.wikipedia.org
www.mlb.com
www.baseballparks.com
www.ballparksofbaseball.com/past/ebbettsfield.htm
www.baseball/national/ebbetts.htm
http://thinkexist.com/quotation
www.baseball-almanac.com/quotes
www.brainyquote.com
www.baseball-reference.com
www.dugoutlegends.com

Ebbet's Field: Brooklyn's Baseball Shrine by Joseph McCauley

The Real Thing (DiMaggio Biography)

www.nydailynews.com
www.historychannel.com
www.deadballera.com
www.baseball-almanac.com
www.baseballhalloffame.org
www.joedimaggio.com
www.baseballprospectus.com
www.sportingnews.com
www.travelwatch.com
www.sethsroom.com
www.en.wikipedia.org
http://goldenrankings.com/dimaggiostreak

A Case for Third Base

www.qcbaseball.com
www.baseball-almanac.com
www.americaninspirational.com
www.cob.ohio-state.edu/tomassin/whotext.html
www.hickoksports.com
www.baseballhalloffame.org
www.cmgww.com
www.nhnhessortment.com
www.deadball.com
www.barberusa.com
www.diamondfans.com
www.whitecleats.org
www.howtooplay.com
www.geocities.com
www.basballlibrary.com
www.truthorfiction.com
www.coachnicko.tripod.com

www.thebasellpage.com
www.writersvoice.org
www.historicbasell.com
www.baseball-reference.com
www.deadera.com
www.baseballcrank.com
www.virtualology.com
www.baseballfantasycamps.com
www.codelikethewind.com
www.veterans.com
www.buffalosportshalloffame.com
www.findarticles.com
http://pittsburgh.pirates.mlb.com/pit/history/retired_numbers.jsp

Baseball and Me

www.baseball-almanac.com/quotes
www.en.wikiquote.org/wiki/field_of_dreams
www.wikipedia.org
http://espn.go.com

Double X (Jimmie Foxx Biography)

www.stream.com
www.tritone.it
www.buzzard_99@yahoo.com
www.baseball-reference.com
www.thebaseballpage.com
www.baseballlibrary.com

---

www.mlb.com

CPSIA information can be obtained at www.ICGtesting.com
Printed in the USA
BVOW06s1246030116

431636BV00002B/87/P